T0399638

Coaching Self-Organising Teams is a valuable contribution to the ever-evolving field of team coaching. Gorell's examples bring to life the intricacies of coaching teams. The tools, philosophies and approaches covered are a great resource for teams, leaders and coaches wanting to amplify their coaching conversations with teams.

> **Jennifer Britton**, Author of *Reconnecting Workspaces and From One to Many: Best Practices for Team and Group Coaching, CEO, Potentials Realized*

Coaching Self-Organising Teams

There is a tendency to assume that teams will naturally know how to self-organise and optimise their collective talents. This thoughtful and engaging book explores the practicalities of coaching teams and some of the challenges that naturally occur because of who we are as human beings.

Part of The Professional Coaching Series, this book challenges the assumption that self-organising teams will work in all settings, answering some of the recurring questions and challenges observed in many organisations. How do we connect with each other, so we create trust? How do we work through conflict and see it as part of a natural ebb and flow in relationships? How do we create meaningful work in the context of an ever-changing environment? The opening chapter lays out some basic team coaching principles to help set the stage for coaching people in teams and there are coaching questions in each chapter to engage the reader as well as tools they can use immediately.

Coaching teams is more than just applying coaching skills. It requires a deep understanding of how people behave and an adaptive approach to coaching. This book provides both research references and practical tools to help team coaches start their team coaching journey.

Ro Gorell is the co-director of Change Optimised, an international consultancy supporting leaders to navigate transformational change. She specialises in organisational change and team coaching, helping organisations through rapid and continuous change, often in challenging environments. She is also a multiple published author on coaching with a best-selling 5th edition of 50 Top Tools For Coaching published in 2021.

The Professional Coaching Series

This series brings together leading exponents and researchers in the coaching field to provide a definitive set of core texts important to the development of the profession. It aims to meet two needs – a professional series that provides the core texts that are theoretically and experimentally grounded, and a practice series covering forms of coaching based in evidence. Together they provide a complementary framework to introduce, promote and enhance the development of the coaching profession.

Titles in the series:

Coaching in Education
Getting Better Results for Students, Educators, and Parents
Christian van Nieuwerburgh

Coaching in the Family Owned Business
A Path to Growth
David A. Lane

Integrated Experiential Coaching
Becoming an Executive Coach
Lloyd Chapman

The Art of Inspired Living
Coach Yourself with Positive Psychology
Sarah Corrie

Coaching Self-Organising Teams
Helping Teams Flourish
Ro Gorell

For further information about this series please visit www.routledge.com/The-Professional-Coaching-Series/book-series/KARNPROFC

Coaching Self-Organising Teams

Helping Teams Flourish

Ro Gorell

Routledge
Taylor & Francis Group

LONDON AND NEW YORK

First published 2022
by Routledge
2 Park Square, Milton Park, Abingdon, Oxon OX14 4RN

and by Routledge
605 Third Avenue, New York, NY 10158

Routledge is an imprint of the Taylor & Francis Group, an informa business

British Library Cataloguing-in-Publication Data
A catalogue record for this book is available from the British Library

Library of Congress Cataloging-in-Publication Data
A catalog record for this book has been requested

ISBN: 978-0-367-62743-0 (hbk)
ISBN: 978-0-367-62745-4 (pbk)
ISBN: 978-1-003-11058-3 (ebk)

DOI: 10.4324/9781003110583

Typeset in Times New Roman
by Apex CoVantage, LLC

Contents

Figures

Tables

Acknowledgements

Thanks to the following for their input, support, guidance, wise words and inspiration.

Yumi Stamet – www.purposeatwork.com.au/
Sergey Helmar
Jason Little – www.leanchange.org
Laurent Prodon
Colart Miles
Richard Scott Will Harknett
Ian Jackson

Thanks to my business partner Charlotte Mawle who has shared many of these learnings with me in the past few years.

Thanks to my husband for reading drafts and generally being there supporting me.

Thanks to Paul Gibbons for agreeing to write the foreword and his words of support and encouragement.

Thanks to our clients who have provided rich learning experiences and inspired me over the years.

Series Editor Foreword
by David A Lane

It is a pleasure to introduce our latest addition to the Professional Coaching Series. As the author contends, the issue of team coaching has created a burgeoning literature in recent years. Academic work in the area is also increasing although the pace is rather slower. At the same time, concepts such as self-organisation, action learning, learning conversations and other related areas have developed. Challenges from the VUCA world and responses such as Agile teams add increasing levels of difficulty in knowing how to respond. In particular, the question of how to decide under conditions of uncertainly becomes more urgent. In bringing these sometimes diverse areas together, the author has provided our readers with intriguing new ways to think about how to operate in complex and rapidly changing environments.

Teamwork has become such an important topic because it is argued that effective teams can drive enhanced performance. Leaders are making decisions in a world of rapidly accessible information, yet the value of those data deteriorates as the world moves on. Leaders have to make decisions without the predictability that previously they sought – 'business needs certainty' is the oft-quoted and increasingly irrelevant cry for many industries. Given constant and shifting contexts, how can leaders decide while ensuring the hierarchies that traditionally enable consistency across all areas of the organisation survive? It seems they cannot. The alternative increasingly proposed is the idea of a common purpose. Where groups of people understand the essence of what they are trying to achieve, it is possible to think creatively without command and control structures. This implies taking qualified risks. But as the author points out to do this, organisations not only need to build shared assumptions but also share their concerns. This provides the context in which teamworking has gained importance. It is particularly the case as remote working has forced new ways for leaders and team members to interact. They may no longer to present in the physical sense but have to be engaged with that common purpose in ways that guides decision making towards its achievement. Trust and autonomy rather than command and control are presented as key currency to underpin the new ways of working.

The difference between a team and a group is explored. This is an area that has provoked much debate and features of this are explored to find a workable definition. However, some of the difficulties with explicit distinctions, for example, looking at senior leadership teams, are acknowledged.

This makes it crucial to understand some of the conditions for team effectiveness. Issues such as clear boundaries and compelling direction are discussed, but the focus of the book is on the role of coaching to achieve valued outcomes.

Yet, while the debate on teams often sees them as self-contained and interdependent, increasingly individuals work across multiple teams each with their own purpose, cultures and structures. This demands a new skill set to flow between different cultures and adapt capabilities developed in one context rapidly to another.

Agile working is seen as one way to achieve this, yet this and related concepts are often presented as good ideas and established within organisational cultures unsuited to such a radical change.

Adopting Agile working without understanding the consequences will result in undesired outcomes. The approach adopted in the book is building self-organising teams (sometimes termed self-directed or autonomous work teams).

This raises a dilemma for which the author offers useful clarification. Can it be assumed that self-organising will grow naturally out of changing contexts or do we need to help team members navigate the journey to trust and autonomy? She argues not only that the skills can be learned but also that some processes can emerge. The practicalities of coaching teams on this path as well as some developments that can naturally occur are explored in detail. The book provides a wealth of ideas to navigation. However, the book is not just for those working in Agile organisations. The value of the approach in any autonomous work team in Agile or non-Agile organisations is examined.

However, to gain most from the book, the author suggests 'adopting a curious mindset and putting preconceived ideas to one side'.

What can you expect from taking this journey with Ro Gorell?

First, the book has been written in a way that you can start at different points focusing on issues that matter to you. Or you can start at the beginning. This provides an accessible and practical way for our readers to get the best from the work. You will be introduced to the idea of systematic curiosity to foster both creativity and constructive conflict. Ro explores understanding the idea that teams are interdependent, whereas groups are collections of individuals. This is a contentious position yet a view that is widely discussed in the coaching literature. In presenting a clear picture of her approach, she enables understanding of where the difference arises and how to make decisions to move between them. This includes exploring the ways coaching for Agile teams works and how this may look different across or even within organisations. Key to this is knowing if your organisation is ready for both coaching and self-organised teams. This leads onto some of the principles which she argues underpin self-organised teams.

These include:

> Self-organising teams do not just happen – you need to look at how it would work for you and why it matters.

Teams can fall into group think – you need to explore how bias in thinking occurs and the ways teams can come to share erroneous ideas because of a common experience.

Conflict is not just something to be avoided but can be beneficial – reframing conflict creatively helps us to explore challenges and the difficult conversations often avoided.

Coaching tools and techniques can be learned – the aim of the coaching is to help generate self-sustaining teams so that as members move on, they can take their experience with them to leverage change elsewhere.

Adaptability can be learned – in this way, teams derive learning from both success and failure.

As organisations change so will the networks within it – teams exist to serve a purpose and when that purpose ends or changes, it is time to understand how to bring it to a 'elegant ending'.

Self-organising teams are excellent when the context in right – this approach is not for everyone or every organisation.

To understand and use the principles outlined in the book, the author suggests keeping notes, reflecting on ideas and practices as you our reader work through the book. This is a practitioner-oriented approach not a research paper. In the same way that the self-organising concept is not for everyone, not all will agree with the author's position on some of the topics. However, she seeks to unpack her thinking in such a way that the readers can make judgements and decide what to take from the book that, importantly, they can apply to their own work as a coach or member of a team. This is a book that will offer something to both coaches of teams and those who work with in them. There is much of value in the book for all.

We are grateful to Ro Gorell for bringing her immense experience to the Professional Coaching Series in such an accessible and practical way. Hence, I am pleased to welcome it as the latest edition to our series.

Professor David A Lane
Professional Development Foundation

Foreword by Paul Gibbons

The holy grail in organisation development and change today is enterprise agility. The challenge is to make businesses both able to handle shocks (such as COVID-19) resiliently and able to seize opportunities more quickly – to be the disruptor rather than the disruptee.

One route to enterprise agility includes self-organising teams. Such teams, research indicates, are more flexible and responsive.

The question then becomes how to form and develop such teams – paradoxically, how does a leader manage such teams? How are parameters and goals set while retaining the team's autonomy and agency? How is performance tracked within the content of self-organisation? How does a self-organising team interact with more structured areas of the business?

These external challenges are matched by internal challenges. To attain the promised levels of higher adaptability and performance, self-organising teams require more extensive development, not less. They require higher levels of trust, greater conflict management skills, more purpose-driven workers, better 'sensing' so that they can be more resilient and a deeper understanding of the role emotions and critical thinking play in solving problems.

In a traditional team, weaknesses in such areas can be papered over. Team conflict can be 'handled' by top-down intervention. Purpose, to a greater extent, is cascaded from senior leadership. Sensing happens through traditional organisation communication siloes and channels.

The challenge Ro Gorell sets herself in Coaching Self-Organising Teams is therefore a mighty and critical one: how are such internal capabilities to be developed without top-down oversight? Some of the questions she answers for readers are:

- How do we discuss, create, maintain and repair trust?
- How do we make conflict a healthy, even a caring experience – one that heals not harms?
- How do we create personal meaning AND shared meaning?
- How do we get stronger through stresses, becoming 'anti-fragile'?
- How do we cope with our emotions in a work setting?
- How can we 'see' ourselves thinking – not just think, but think about how we think?

Coaching Self-Organising Teams (CSOT) is written through the lens of a 'team coach' who helps teams reach standards of adaptability and build the skills and mindset to self-organise. However, there are thousands of books written by consultant/coaches on the well-travelled topic of teams. What differentiates Ro's work is her critical eye on what academics have had to say on relevant topics: trust, complexity, psychological safety, conflict and so on.

This makes CSOT a rich read – not just full of tips and tools but replete with justifications for why those tools are essential and how they work.

I believe that the book will be one of the essential leadership 'must-reads' of this decade and commend it to you heartily.

Paul Gibbons
June 2021, Colorado

Introduction

Setting the scene and introducing the core premise of the book: self-organising teams don't just happen on their own

Organisations looking for an edge are increasingly adopting 'Agile' ways of working. This often means introducing new approaches into an existing organisational system often without doing due diligence to understand if the organisation is ready for the change and second, without understanding the consequences of the approach. One of these approaches is self-organising teams which has been popularised by the rise of 'digital transformations' and all things related to 'The Digital Age'. Those readers from a non-Agile background may be more familiar with the terms self-directed or autonomous work teams.

There is a tendency in organisations to assume that teams and groups will naturally know how to self-organise and optimise their collective talents. This book aims to explore the practicalities of coaching teams and some of the challenges that naturally occur. It will also explore tips, tools and techniques to help you navigate this fascinating and rewarding subject.

The focus of the book is on coaching self-organising teams in organisations' both Agile and non-Agile environments. It is written, hopefully, in a way that can be applied to any type of autonomous work group – more on definitions later. Essentially if you're working with a group of people, there are some common principles and foundations that apply across the board. Together we'll explore what these are and hopefully along the way you'll gain some specific insights about how these broad principles and foundations might apply to your organisation.

One of the core principles we'll explore is transparency. To be transparent, this book outlines some simple hypotheses drawn from experience of working with people in teams and groups, tempered with research and evidence. If you have a particular model that you're tied to, it might be worth adopting a curious mindset and putting preconceived ideas to one side as we explore together the usefulness of models and frameworks. Challenging our thinking is part of helping teams become curious and learn together. Some of the models in my previously published books have been updated and challenged to deepen thinking about what works, what doesn't and why.

Coaching teams inevitably raises some common questions. If you are reading this book because you are tasked with coaching teams to help them learn how to self-organise, you may be familiar with some of the frequently asked questions:

DOI: 10.4324/9781003110583-1

- How do we connect with each other, so we create trust?
- How do we work through conflict and see it as part of a natural ebb and flow in relationships?
- How do we create meaningful work in the context of an ever-changing environment?
- How do we develop resilience, so we can flex as the organisation flexes?
- How do we cope with our human emotions in a work setting?
- How can we gain a better understanding of our thinking?

Systematic curiosity

Experimentation and a growth mindset are two other core principles that seem to help groups free their thinking about how they work together and foster creativity and constructive conflict. This is what I call systematic curiosity. At its heart is the concept of hypothesis creation in the form of declarative statements. To be clear, these are not objective statements, more opinion-based declarations to be explored and viewed from different perspectives.

Over the course of the book, we will dive into them individually within the chapters. Here's a brief overview so that you know what to expect as you read through the book. How you read this book is up to you. Finding a chapter that strikes a chord or covers a topic you're grappling with is one way. Of course, you can also read it cover to cover; either way, each chapter provides a small summary and some quick tips on key takeaways.

Groups are collections of independent members; teams are interdependent

There are basic principles that apply to both and some differences. Clarity on what constitutes a team and what constitutes a group helps create boundaries and scope for who to coach. Defining what is in scope for the coaching also helps. Delineating coaching from mentoring and where the lines might blur forms part of the co-creation process. It follows that the coach needs to understand the difference and know when they might be moving from one to the other. And whether or not that is OK.

Agile coaching means different things to different organisations, therefore an exploration of some of the ways Agile coaches work helps create a landscape to map out where you sit as a coach and, on that point, understanding if your organisation is ready for coaching and self-organising teams. Identifying some of the key foundation stones that probably need to be in place first is where we'll start.

Having explored that, we'll look at some of the basic principles around coaching people in self-sustaining teams and what might be similar or different depending on the types of teams you're coaching, for example, technical based teams or non-technical teams as well as the type of frameworks your organisation might be adopting.

Self-organising teams don't just happen on their own

Organisations looking at leveraging teams have to work out the practicalities of making it work, for example, the scope for decision making, the scope of work, tasks and process; how to co-create – the tools and techniques; the contracting process within the team – simple things from 'what's my role in the team?' to the more complex domain of 'how can we develop trust in the team?' and both the physical and psychological contracting process of co-creating a safe space.

Trust is often cited as one of the most important things, either overtly or tacitly when working in teams. Ensuring the team sets itself up for progress at the beginning of the relationship enables them to create resilience when things get tough or minds get tired.

We also know the importance of predictability and perception of control, so gaining clarity on how long the team plans to work together and how much say individual members have in this ensures a greater degree of psychological safety and assists with pacing work.

Teams often fall into the trap of group think

It takes conscious effort to leverage ideas and deep thinking in teams because of our natural biases and thinking habits (heuristics). Humans are not rational – even though we like to think we are! Adopting a behavioural economist mindset to working with teams ensures that we explore the likely biases at play. It is understanding that there will also be natural rules of thumb that we use to make decisions. Helping the group explore these in a meaningful way, whilst acknowledging that this is what makes us human, forms part of the toolkit for coping with conflict.

Some of the tools at the coach's disposal are based on 'thinking slow' – purposeful or deliberate practice, reflection and retrospectives.

Working through conflict is healthy if teams are to succeed

Our instincts often lead us to conflict avoidance. There are tactics for working through conflict to harness its creative rather than destructive force. Often teams shy away from difficult topics or avoid conflict which eventually leads to more conflict. Undeclared grievances build, leading to tension and eventual explosion.

Understanding the nature of conflict and what it is means, we can help teams explore a necessary part of our humanness and from which creativity can flow. Moreover, reframing this into creative conflict rather than destructive conflict helps the team grow both individually and together. We build on our contracting process here to help the team explore challenges and discover how to have healthy debate through tools such as reframes, perspectives mapping and perceptual positions.

Group coaching tools and techniques can be learnt

The role of the coach is to hand over the coaching process to the team at a predetermined time in the future. Learning by doing is one of the core principles, and the role of the coach is to ensure that the team has the capability to be self-sustaining in every sense. Having an armoury of tools and techniques at a team's disposal enables self-sustainment. And these tools are portable for work with other groups and teams. Coaching self-sustaining teams is a ripple effect – as each team member moves to a new team, they take their experiences with them and can leverage the learning throughout the organisation as they coach others to coach.

Building on some of the tools created in my book on Group Coaching, Kogan Page (2013), I share some ways to develop your own tools as well as sharing some of the core tools I have used in my practice to help teams.

Adaptability is a learned skill. Resilience helps flex the muscle

Coaching people in groups helps develop skills in self-organising and flexibility. Having the support of others helps foster resilience. Inevitably, there will be times when the team has to push through a particularly testing challenge. These are defining moments of growth. Coaching helps the team derive learning from both success and failure in equal measure. Coping with change is the watchword.

Helping the team understand what's within their control and what isn't is about contextualising and making sense of the change. The concept of growth mindset supports resilience and encourages experimentation and innovation. This is where we revisit the notion of psychological safety and forms the bedrock of self-sustaining teams. A reality check on the context is also important because what might be safe within the confines of the team might not be in the wider context of the organisation.

All good things come to an end

And maybe not so good things depending on how the team has worked together. As organisations change, so will the networks of people within. Knowing when the group/team has served its purpose enables growth. Here we explore the contract to understand over what timeframe the team is working and the concept of elegant endings, much like the coaching conversation – a check in on where you are now compared with where you started. Team members can often feel like family members, so it is important to understand our needs as human beings to acknowledge our need to connect and make sense of the natural ebb and flow.

Tools to help with this process are the retrospective and storytelling canvas, capturing learning and insights both for the team members and for the organisation.

Self-organising teams aren't for everyone. Context is king

Self-organising teams might be a future aspiration for traditional hierarchical organisations. Having explored the hypotheses, it is important to acknowledge where we started. Doing due diligence on whether self-organising teams is appropriate for your organisation is key. This responsibility sits outside the scope of the coach but forms part of the qualification process.

Examining the evidence that supports the value and benefit of self-organising teams is essential if your teams are to be set for success and progress. Whilst it might be the fashionable thing at the time of writing this book in 2021, it might not be the wisest thing to embark on. A cautionary note for traditional hierarchical organisations – self-organising teams will seriously challenge your management systems and management hierarchy. Think carefully before you set course for a choppy and turbulent journey.

Getting started

Bias to action is sometimes a good thing. I encourage you to write notes as you read through the chapters, perhaps dividing your page into two columns with one column titled 'what resonates' and the other column titled 'what jars'. Whilst I have approached this topic with an evidence-based mindset, it is not an academic research paper, more a practitioner's workbook. The hypotheses explored earlier will be unpacked and discussed in more detail allowing you to draw your own conclusions.

There is a bibliography at the end of each chapter, which refers to the material quoted or inferred in the text plus other resources that formed part of my research and included for completion so you can explore the topics for yourself. Whilst I recognise this is not normal practice, I've added in the spirit of being helpful.

Insights over inspiration is one of my coaching mantras so that you sustain your own learning as you coach others the same.

Chapter 1

Team coaching and self-organising teams

The basic principles and context

My early experience of coaching teams ignited a spark of curiosity and got me thinking. What is the special ingredient that makes some teams flourish? How can we help teams make the leap from ordinary to extraordinary? How does our coaching help or hinder the team? And why is teamwork so essential? Searching for answers to these questions has been a challenging and enlightening journey over the last two and a half decades.

And, if you are coaching teams and have the same burning desire to understand what makes the difference, please read on.

The topic of teams and teamwork has propagated hundreds of articles and books in the last few decades alone – a Google search for the word 'teamwork' yields around 132,000,000 results. Teamwork is now a hot topic. The extent of research on teamwork also suggests the increasing interest from both academics and organisations. Why has teamwork become so important? It is the belief that it can lead to increased business performance and better outcomes. The question is how to convert this belief into reality.

Spend a few minutes thinking about where you work. How much change have you personally experienced at work in the last decade? The answer will likely be a significant amount of change, especially if you work in an organisation reliant on technology.

In the last two decades, we have seen technology advance beyond what we thought possible. The computing power in your phone exceeds the computing power that landed humans on the moon! (Kendall 2019). Given this change in technology and the pervasive effect on our lives, small wonder that organisations realise leveraging teamwork is a sensible way to meet head-on the inevitable challenge ahead, including complexity and uncertainty.

Complexity is a challenge in most organisations arising out of the increasing pace of change and shifting contexts. For leaders, this means grappling with making decisions on the unknown unknowns (Snowden and Boone 2007) – this is the crucial differentiator of leadership versus management. Leaders make decisions where there are no known precedents, whereas managers decide using precedents and previous good or best practice. Action taken in one part of the organisation might have implications and consequences for seemingly unrelated

DOI: 10.4324/9781003110583-2

areas in a different part of the organisation. Complex problems also require different speeds of decision making. It is no longer practical to wait for decisions to be made higher up the 'chain of command'. In this context, having a group of people working together towards a common purpose makes sense. One where to think creatively, take qualified risks and share assumptions and concerns is encouraged and supported.

And so, the scene is set for why teams and teamworking have gained increasing importance. There has always been volatility, uncertainty, complexity and ambiguity in the world. Think back to any time in history, and examples will come to mind. The difference now is the pace at which this happens. The same technology we value has increased the speed of change because new emerging technologies disrupt previously stable industries. We are now globally connected at the touch of a button. Information flows across the world, and remote areas are connected in real time. We no longer must wait for information – it is there, at our fingertips in an instant.

At the date of writing, we face a pandemic that saw many organisations rush to find ways of connecting employees remotely so that they could continue working from home in the space of a few weeks. During 2020, we have seen technological changes advance because of the pandemic – projects that were at the inception stage were fast-tracked to ensure survival and sustainability. Some organisations introduced Microsoft Teams in the space of three weeks – something which typically takes months. The advent of reliable and cheap video conferencing tools such as Zoom and Skype meant employees could work anywhere. In my own business, my business partner and I pivoted a face-to-face workshop into an online learning experience using Zoom and an online learning platform to ensure that we could continue to deliver during the COVID lockdown.

The reality of remote working forced autonomous working and confronted many organisations that operated a more traditional hierarchical model. In a remote online world, managers could no longer 'check up' on employees to see if they were doing what they should. Trust, therefore, became valuable currency conjoined with autonomy.

In this context, the pace of change has led, if not driven, organisations to seek better ways of working and leveraging their resources, including people. Teams and teamwork are a way of creating choice and cognitive diversity – if done well! The subject of this book is how to blend these, so the whole is greater than merely the sum of the parts.

1.1 What is a team?

In researching this book, it became apparent that these four words have generated hundreds of books, research, discussion, arguments and counterarguments. Such is the enthusiasm for the quest. The follow-on question, 'why does this matter?', is perhaps more important for the coach working with a 'team'.

First, let us explore what constitutes a team. How will the organisation know if it has created a 'real team' or a group? The simplest explanation of what constitutes a teal team comes from the research of Michael West and colleagues working with the U.K. National Health Service, particularly in health and social care. He outlines three prerequisites for a real team:

- Clear, shared objectives
- Working closely together
- Meets regularly to review and improve performance

Building on the work of West, I offer some key questions to consider when determining if the organisation is creating a group or team.

If there is little interdependence and collective accountability, and no shared purpose, the organisation likely creates a group of people rather than a team. Again, a simple definition of a group is a collection of people who report to the same function or manager. In organisational terms, this is usually the reporting line on an organisation chart. The link between the individuals is merely the fact that they report through the same structure with individual accountabilities and contributions. The exception to this might be at the senior executive level. Typically, executive team members have discrete responsibility for a business unit and collective responsibility to deliver business-wide results. Delivering business-wide results does not necessarily mean that the executive team will be a real team – given the explanation earlier about complexity, it is increasingly likely that more executive teams will now have to function as real teams (Wageman et al. 2008).

Table 1.1 Prerequisites for Real Teams

Prerequisite	
Shared purpose	What are we here to do?
	What are the outcomes we are seeking to achieve?
	Why does that matter?
Interdependency	What can only be done by collaborating?
	What can be done individually?
	What additional outcomes will be achieved by working together?
Collective accountability	What must we achieve together?
	How often will we review progress?
	What will happen outside of meetings?
	What will happen if one individual does not meet the requirements?
Drive to improve	What time will be spent on reflecting on progress and learning?
	How will the learning be applied to future work together?
	What level of willingness is there to allow space for reflection?

What constitutes a team and team effectiveness elide in most research. Hackman (2002) expounds five conditions for team effectiveness, and we can see some overlap with the themes mentioned earlier on defining teams:

1 Clear boundaries – they know what they are there to do
2 Compelling direction focused on ends rather than means
3 Structure, team makeup, standards of conduct
4 Shared support system
5 Competent coaching

As is apparent, these conditions also indicate some of the critical characteristics of what constitutes a team – with the final condition being the core subject of this book, coaching.

Team fluidity is also a topic gaining importance given that teams become more relevant in an ever-changing and complex economy. Teaming, a concept outlined by Edmondson (2012, 2013), considers the dynamics of responding to situations as they arise. The ability to flex and adapt suggests that teaming as an activity requires a skillset ready, willing and able to work with others as the need arises. Edmondson makes the point that individuals no longer work in just one team. They may belong to multiple teams, and the ability to ebb and flow with different teams requires an entirely different set of skills and capabilities.

Edmondson and Harvey (2017) call this ability to team 'extreme teaming' and identify four functions:

1 Building an engaging vision
2 Cultivating psychological safety
3 Develop shared mental models
4 Empower Agile execution

Their research provides some great insights into how these functions are practically applied in the organisations they researched. Later, we will explore how these themes naturally crop up in teams. If you have been working with teams, either as a coach or as part of a team, you will no doubt nod your head in agreement at the first three. The last one perhaps has become more popular because of the word Agile. However, for many who have worked in business improvement, this will also come as no surprise.

Many organisations moved to a matrix structure back in the late 90s. The ability to work well with other people and achieve business outcomes was a continual challenge. Organisations that had previously relied on stable hierarchical structures grappled with the shift in working practices and the challenge to established bureaucracy. Teams were expected to work together without much support, but the leadership also grappled with leading in this 'new world' of changing reporting lines and accountabilities. The siloed business units stymie fluidity. The teams lost valuable time arguing internal rules and procedures instead of focusing on customers and how the teams would work to deliver value.

Edmondson and Harvey's research sheds new light on what it means to create teams when organisations need to shift their operating model. The inclusion of psychological safety is an essential addition to facets of teamwork. Building on the commentary mentioned earlier, that ability to work 'cross-boundary' (Edmondson and Harvey 2017) underpins the reason for teaming in current organisations. During the current pandemic, the world is figuring out how to work across boundaries in organisations and countries. Helping teams develop teaming instincts requires the ability to involve a broader audience in the team's work. Taking a more comprehensive stakeholder perspective is true teaming activity and touches on the systemic nature of teams – they exist in the broader context that includes the organisation, external stakeholders and the environment in which the organisation operates.

Coaching teams to become self-organising therefore takes on greater importance if organisations are to embed 'teaming' skills for business benefit. We will explore some examples of organisations that embody this approach later.

I have attempted to map the conditions and characteristics of a team in the following map and source.

We have touched briefly on the concept of complexity and how the function of shared mental models relates to this. Making sense together of what we are doing and how we are doing it underpins this function. The role of a leader is also vital in orchestrating this. Self-organising teams don't just happen overnight. Therefore, the coach must understand how they work with the team and the leadership to support its development and evolution.

Table 1.2 Conditions and Characteristics of Teams

Purpose and Direction	Context	Process
• Compelling purpose • Goal clarity • Team members motivated by purpose and goal • Team sees value in purpose and direction • Team member needs and wants taken into account • Collective team needs considered	• Resources allocated – time, money, people, equipment, energy, capacity • Developing learning as a skillset • Organisation system supports collaboration and teamwork • Focus on satisfying customer needs and wants	• Team responsible for planning and structuring tasks • Communication – formal and informal • Clear team scope and delegated authority • Defined processes for how the team works together and interacts with the organisation • Clear who does what • Team membership criteria clear – including time allocation for everyone for each team they are part of

Collaboration	Roles	Team Composition
• Shared agenda – individual team members advocate for team agenda over individual agenda • Individual members motivated to support each other • Team members demonstrate genuine caring • Team leverages all team members' talents • Individual team members valued for unique contribution	• Clarity • Matched to skills • Leader role – part of the team or external to the team? • Role modelling – to the team and the organisation • Leadership functions – distributed • Sponsor/commissioner of the team	• Team selection – who decides? • Cross function or single function – depending on the level of complexity • Team boundaries clear – team membership clear • Exclusively member of one team or member of multiple teams

Behaviour	Task	Team Type
• Team norms – acceptable versus unacceptable behaviours • Bias towards helping • Willingness to engage in challenging dialogue • Psychological safety • Resilience – ability to go back to form • Openness to – knowledge acquisition, other's experience, insight and curiosity • Able to cope with and recognise conflict as a natural process of team development	• Clear task structure – sub-tasks, no duplication, no gaps • High task interdependence • Collective task accountability • Performance standards agreed and process for renegotiation clear in complex environments • Task related to stakeholder context	• Self-organising • Team-leader led • Self-designing • Ad hoc • Durability of team over time – if a stable team • Ability to team quickly if ad hoc • Cross function or single function depending on the complexity and scope

The final function of empowering Agile execution fits well in a complex environment since it includes 'safe to fail probes' (Snowden) or 'execution as learning' (Edmondson and Harvey). Teaming consists of autonomy in this function since it recognises experts' ability to make decisions.

No discussion on teams can be complete without including the research carried out by Google on its Aristotle project (Rozovsky 2015). Google analysed thousands of data to understand what made teams in Google successful. The top indicator of team success was psychological safety. This research probably catapulted Edmondson's original research in the 90s to instant fame. The other indicators of team success were dependability – that is, can you rely on your teammates to do what they say they will do? Will they have your back? Structure and clarity also featured in the success indicators and the meaning of work, and the impact of work.

- Psychological safety
- Dependability
- Structure and clarity
- Meaning of work
- Impact of work

The Google research underpinned some of the themes from previous research. Look back at the three critical facets of what constitutes a real team from West, and many of the Google success indicators can be intertwined. For example, you can't work closely with teammates if there isn't underlying trust and support, which comes from psychological safety and dependability.

I have attempted to give a brief overview of some of the available research. The corollary quest – 'why does this matter?' is hopefully becoming clearer. Coaching teams first requires that we are working with a team, not a group. The approach taken with coaching groups is different from teams. Coaching a team is about helping the team to work interdependently – to work in a way that achieves a shared outcome and objective to which each subscribes. The coach co-creates ways in which the team can learn this together to become capable of self-organising.

Moreover, they become able to coach each other (peer-to-peer coaching) and coach others to do the same. The concept of teaming aligns with self-organising teams. It provides the coach with an opportunity to develop and co-create approaches to help the team and the organisation work towards a self-organising system capable of flexing to changing demands and requirements.

1.2 What is a self-organising team?

This question has raised much debate and discussion, with many valuable research papers and articles exploring the concept of self-organisation. The question also poses more detailed questions about how self-organising teams come into being. The reality is that self-organising teams do not just happen on their own. There have to be conditions under which they can flourish. The role of leaders is crucial in setting the climate for both teams and self-organisation. As mentioned earlier, teams and teamwork are more complex than first appears before adding teaming as an activity. First, we need to understand what self-organising means. An understanding of self-organising leads to a discussion of the role of leaders. The following terms seem to be used frequently synonymously with the notion of self-organisation:

- Self-directed
- Self-managed
- Self-managed natural workgroup or team
- Autonomous workgroup

In defining self-organisation, it is helpful to call out that self-managed work teams are sometimes associated with holacratic organisation structures. Holacracy was born out of the work of Frederic Laloux (2014). In short, holacracy is a model for distributed power within the organisation that removes hierarchy and focuses on autonomy, agility and a purpose-driven framework. It is radical in concept and confronting in its application through the removal of traditional hierarchy. Self-organising teams can thrive in more traditional organisations and without moving to a holacracy model. SCRUM (Sutherland and Schwaber 1995) is self-organising and operates effectively within organisations that employ a more traditional organisation structure. We will explore the challenges and benefits of adopting a wholesale self-organised structure within an organisation in a later chapter. For now, the focus is on what is meant by self-organised teams.

One of the possible reasons self-organising teams have gained popularity is the renewed and rising interest in Agile. As mentioned earlier, SCRUM – a framework for software development projects – has brought it into everyday conversations. Recently, more organisations are adopting SCRUM principles for non-IT-related projects. The increased interest in Agile working partly explains why the term is now becoming so popular. Here's what the Agile Manifesto says concerning teams:

'The best architectures, requirements, and designs emerge from self-organizing teams'.

Agile Principle, Agile Manifesto (2001)

By way of a slight detour, here's a brief introduction to Agile for those not familiar. Back in 2000, there was a rush to create the latest dot com business. In February and May 2000, I had the opportunity to visit some of these startups in Silicon Valley and Boston. Working for a large corporation, these nimble and creative startups were very inviting and excited the innovator within me. Working for a large I.T. organisation, I knew firsthand the challenges we were facing. We were not alone. Many Information Technology companies were faced with an increasing drive to create flexible and faster solutions for clients that relied on technology solutions partly catalysed by these small but numerous dot com startups.

By the end of 2000, many startups based on technology solutions had faltered, and the dot com bubble burst. Developing software solutions could be a time-consuming and costly exercise. The cost factor created challenges for larger organisations because the lead time from initiation to implementation was long and often did not consider changing requirements that naturally occur over a long time duration. Once the development process started, it was difficult to change course as customer requirements shifted and any changes in the wider external environment. For example, if government regulations or standards changed during a development phase, this could disrupt the whole development lifecycle, meaning re-work and cost escalation.

In February 2001, a group of software developers met and, in their quest to make the software development experience better, created the Agile Manifesto.

The Manifesto contains four values and 12 principles which include the principle of self-organising teams. Self-organising teams was not a new concept, but the link with I.T. architectures, requirements and design, challenged existing norms. Linking human factors into an I.T. paradigm questioned the received wisdom about technology teams. That human behaviour and interaction should feature so prominently in the Agile Manifesto indicates why helping teams improve their work together is essential. This assertion has led to a whole industry of practices, methods and tools designed to support such teams, with SCRUM being the most favoured and frequently adopted framework.

Therefore, it is easy to fall into the trap of thinking that self-organising teams are a relatively new phenomenon, they are not. Reg Revans (2011) created the concept of self-directed teams and the practice of action learning. In 1994, I learned this approach whilst working for a Telco company – one of the first to emerge after the de-nationlisation of the telecoms industry in the U.K. Quality Circles came out of the Quality Movement and popularised by the Just-in-time methods introduced by Toyota as described by Ishikawa (1985) and adopted by other manufacturers. Quality circles were popular in the 1980s with the Quality Movement and partly driven by changes in automation within the manufacturing industry.

Self-organising can mean a range of things. In this context, we will use the following principles to help qualify self-organising distinct from a traditional team where the leader regulates and manages the work for the team:

- Assigning tasks – the team can work out how to set the tasks and responsibilities within the team.
- Decision making – the team can make decisions concerning how they do the work.
- Behavioural norms – the team creates their standards of behaviour to self-govern.
- Autonomy and self-direction – the team is autonomous and self-motivated towards the common goal.
- Scope of authority – the team operates within the bounds of the broader organisation. The organisation will likely set the boundaries and rules of engagement.

In addition to these principles, self-organising teams will also have what we will loosely term a set of responsibilities:

- A degree of autonomy – how much will depend on the organisation
- To plan work within the team free from external direction
- To create processes for working together as a team
- Self-regulating for completion of tasks, i.e. relying on team members to do what they say they will do and holding them to account if they don't
- Collective responsibility for producing an output or outcome

The work of Francis Heylighen, an expert in the field of science and physics, sheds some further light on self-organising (1970). He identifies certain traits exhibited by self-organising systems. The core traits relevant to human systems and self-organising teams are:

- Lack of centralised control
- Adaptation to an environment in flux
- Resilience to regroup and repair
- Response to feedback – positive and negative
- Emergence of structure from disorder

The organisation itself becomes the container in which this self-organisation takes place, and the teams that exist within this container become independent yet connected to the whole.

Heylighen explains that some traits are universal to self-organising systems. One of these is the lack of centralised control. Another trait, continuous adaptation to an environment in flux, is exhibited only by complex eco-systems. Since human systems are by nature complex, it suggests that a self-organising team will have an ability to adapt to change – creating a learning system as opposed to a closed one. This particular trait has an interesting and helpful implication for the coach working with a team. It implies that part of the function of a coach is to help the team learn to harness this adaptability. Learning is part of adaptation, and later we will explore some practical ways of assisting teams in understanding what this means and create a learning system for practical application.

Hackman (2002) explores self-organisation from the perspective of governance. This perspective aligns well with the concept of team commissioning and setting of boundaries and provides the coach with a language to start a conversation on self-organisation with both leaders and teams. Returning to the concept of 'real teams' as distinct from workgroups, Hackman describes the four characteristics:

1   Task – the team works on the task or tasks interdependently. The task cannot be completed without the individuals working together.
2   Boundaries – the critical boundary is knowing who is in the team. For Hackman, a real team has stable membership.
3   Authority – clarity on what decisions the team can and cannot make. Delegated authority is essential for real teams, but not at the expense of overstepping the bounds of decision-making authority.
4   Stability – a critical distinction that teams must work together over time so that they learn.

> Adapted and reprinted with permission from 'Leading Teams: Setting the Stage for Great Performances' by J. Richard Hackman. Harvard Business Press Books, 2002.

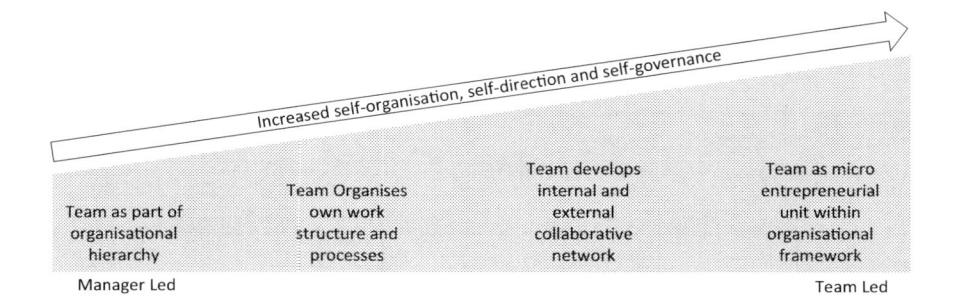

Team as part of organisational hierarchy	Team Organises own work structure and processes	Team develops internal and external collaborative network	Team as micro entrepreneurial unit within organisational framework

Manager Led .... Team Led

Figure 1.1 Towards Self-Organisation

There is a gradient of self-organisation from one end where managers lead teams to the other where teams self-govern. To help coaches understand if they are working with a self-organising team, the team governance will likely be along the gradient from self-managing to self-governing. We mentioned SCRUM as one of the Agile methods, and an organisation using this approach is likely to be adopting self-designing teams, based on Hackman's assessment. Self-governing teams in Hackman's work are executive boards, legislative bodies and professional partnerships. In organisations adopting a holacracy model, self-organising teams will likely sit more towards the end of the gradient – self-governing teams.

The diagram at Figure 1.1 provides a simplified model of manger-led versus team-led teams. At the extreme, team-led teams will likely operate as micro entrepreneurial units within an organisation framework. It might be useful to perceive the organisation as a holding company model in this model.

Let us return to the concept of teaming versus real teams. The key difference is around team stability – that teams need to work together to leverage and improve their efficiency and effectiveness effectively. The evidence presented by Edmondson and Harvey is convincing – that teams must work together more flexibly and at speed, focusing on learning to collaborate quickly. Let's take Hackman's three other conditions for real teams and add in the dimension of speed suggested by Edmondson and Harvey. We can see how effective team coaching can assist teams in operating in the world of complexity and uncertainty. For those readers familiar with Hackathons and Startup weekends, you will recognise the importance of teaming as a concept and skill. Imagine you have two days to take an idea from inception to production with live customers for those not familiar with hackathons and startup weekends. All the time working with people you've just met, with different skillsets and personalities. Throw into the mix an element of competition, and you will realise this mirrors the world we live in today.

Leading to the critical question and proposition behind this book – how can coaches help self-organising teams leverage their value and become self-sustaining? If we consider that organisations are complex systems, the people who work there need to respond to emerging needs and changes. As the previous brief illustration suggests, market volatility and the ability to adapt and respond quickly are normal in many industries. Self-organising makes sense if your organisation is coping with this fast-paced change. It takes too long for information to flow up and down the organisation from those higher up the chain of command who don't always have sufficient detailed knowledge of the area. Delegating this authority throughout the organisation and putting flexible and responsive governance practices in place provides a competitive advantage and makes the work more meaningful for the people who 'live' in the organisation. Agility and the ability to respond and innovate mean more organisations will move towards self-organising teams.

1.3 Why context matters – self-organising teams might not work everywhere

Adopting an approach just because it is popular is not a sound strategy. The heuristic that 'if others are doing it, it must make sense' can be a seductive path to follow. However, we know from recent experiences that organisations have adopted a particular organisation model to discover it doesn't fit their context. The 'model de jour' in the Agile world is the 'Spotify model'. What this model is and how it works specifically cannot be described because it is organic and morphs and changes depending on the context within Spotify. Spotify employees have given talks on the fact that there is no Spotify model (2016). The lure of agility still captures many organisations who falsely believe that they will succeed if they can do what Spotify does.

This myth prevails in organisations seeking to move towards self-organising teams. Find a case study we can emulate, and all will be well. Instead, first, understand where you're starting from and proceed from there. Before beginning any coaching assignment, there is a consultancy pre-phase whereby we ask the client – either internal or external – some of the following questions in Table 1.3.

The questions are designed to start the thinking process, and you should add your own based on your own experiences. Coaching self-organising teams is a process of co-discovery. Helping the organisation explore different paths to a possible future is part of the engagement process you as a coach will undertake. As you can see, team coaching might mean adopting more of a consulting style in the early stages to help your client understand their context. Coaching self-organising teams means taking a wider perspective on all the stakeholders and co-creates understanding about what might work and the appetite for experimentation to see what the organisation is open to trying. It also forms part of the foundation of coaching teams – if the context is not going to support self-organisation, perhaps a different approach to teaming is required.

Creating a direction of travel towards the future end goal makes more sense when working in complexity and uncertainty rather than having a fixed endpoint. Self-organising teams, by their nature, will initially be unpredictable. Still, as the team learns and evolves, a pattern of behaviours will emerge, which will provide

Table 1.3 Towards Self-Organisation

Characteristic	Questions
Delegated authority	How far are we willing to delegate authority?
	What specific types of decisions can be made at the team level?
	What specific types of decisions must be referred to the manager?
Boundaries	How will the team membership be decided?
	How will changes in the team be decided?
	What types of skills will be important?
	Will there be skill groupings or diversity?
	Will skillsets be important?
	How will cognitive and cultural diversity in the team be achieved? What type of diversity is required?
	Where are the potential team members situated in the organisation currently?
Task	What is the task the team(s) will be working?
	How much interdependence is required for task completion?
Stability/ fluidity	How long will the team work together?
	How many teams will one individual belong to?
	How will teams be created and disbanded?
	Who will decide on the creation and disbandment of the team?
Context	What is the overall organisational purpose that self-organisation supports?
	What is the existing context?
	How challenging will be the move to self-organisation?
	What might the organisation need to let go?
	What might the organisation need to keep?
	How will we know if it's been successful?
	What will be the measures of success?

a cadence of working together that creates sustainability. It will become apparent whether or not the organisation is going in the right direction or veering off course into a different future.

Any organisation wishing to adopt self-organising teams must be prepared for an initial stage of confusion and be on board for the work ahead. Transitioning from leader-led teams to self-organising teams is one of those bridges to cross and the subject of the next piece of the contextual puzzle.

1.4 The role of leaders in self-organising teams

When we coach teams moving towards self-organisation, there will likely be an existing hierarchical model in play. This model means that there will be a team leader or manager responsible for the team. To help work with the teams and their leaders, let's explore leadership first and then work within the different leadership contexts.

Different theories of leadership have developed over the years. Many trait-based models focus on leadership characteristics and behaviours. In his book, Pfeffer (2015) describes some of the drawbacks of these models. The model most helpful for coaching teams is a functional leadership model. This model sees leadership as a function of meeting the team's needs to execute its goal. The particular model we will explore is outlined in Morgeson et al.'s paper (2010). They outline 15 functions divided into two phases – one phase when the team is set up and the second phase when the team is doing the work.

They go on to examine who is best placed to help the team with these activities.

The key to this model of leadership is the focus on the activity, not the role. There are potentially multiple sources of leadership that can come from within the team or outside the team and can be either formal or informal. This model is a distributed leadership model and fits well within the context of self-organisation. It illustrates that the team can lead itself or source others to help – a team coach is one example. Other examples are team sponsors, advisors, mentors and project managers. Here's a snapshot of the leadership functions with short descriptions.

Table 1.4 Leadership Functions

Team Setup		*Team Performance*	
Leadership Function	*Description*	*Leadership Function*	*Description*
Compose team	Team selection, compatibility, capability	Monitor team	Measuring progress, available outcomes, external factors and team members
Define mission	Clarity on what the team is there to do – tangible and easy to understand	Manage team boundaries	Manage the opposing demands of internal and external boundaries so that the team can be protected from but still exchange information with wider environment
Establish expectations and goals	Clarity on performance required and team development	Challenge team	Confronting assumptions, methods and process and encouraging different styles of thinking
Structure and plan	Clarity on how the team will achieve their goals including likely methods, roles and responsibilities, scheduling and workflow	Perform team task	Helping the team get things done
Train and develop team	Clarity on how the team will increase capabilities and collaborative practices	Solve problems	Leveraging the team's combined expertise and knowledge to assess resolve and implement solutions

(Continued)

Table 1.4 (Continued)

Team Setup		Team Performance	
Leadership Function	Description	Leadership Function	Description
Sensemaking	Making sense of events outside the team and developing adaptive practices to create resilience and flexibility	Provide resources	Obtaining resources needed to complete the task including technical, financial, informational and people resources
Provide feedback	Reviewing progress on tasks, ability and goal achievement with purpose of continual development	Encourage team self-management	Encourage the team to perform its own leadership function in the creation of autonomous work structure
		Support social climate	Helping the team create a positive work environment that fosters social cohesion

Source: Adapted and reprinted with permission from 'Leadership in Teams: A Functional Approach to Understanding Leadership Structures and Processes', Frederick Morgesen et al. *Journal of Management*, vol. 36, no. 1, Jan. 2010, pp. 5–39.

Team coaches perform some of these leadership functions in helping the team meet some of these needs. Which functions the team coach helps with will depend on when the coaching assignment starts. The functional leadership model is a great reference tool for team coaches because it helps us name what's happening within the team and point us to coaching strategies. For example, solving problems can be a sticking point for teams. Using the functional leadership model, we can co-create coaching interventions to help the team combine its expertise. Similarly, we can encourage team members to take ownership of different parts of the coaching sessions to practice self-management. Later in the book, we will explore some of the ways of doing this.

The functional model of leadership can also help leaders transition to a model of self-organising teams. Freed from the hierarchical constraints or the role and focusing more on the function of leadership allows leaders to transition to more of a coaching role. Yumi Stamet, a coach/mentor to self-organising team coaches, working in the social care sector, describes some of the challenges for leaders moving to a self-organised model. Even where leaders are keen to support self-organising teams and embrace a coaching role, the IT Systems are set up based on a hierarchical structure. This structure means that tasks in the transition phase outside the delegated authority of the teams have to be completed by the leader/coach, for example, shift swaps and leave. The leader/coach has to perform some administrative and governance functions because the management system is catching up with the new ways of working. Typically, the leader role in her experience is usually transformed into the coach role, making it difficult in the early phases for the leader to perform the coaching role because they still have the responsibilities for performing some of these hygiene factors for the team.

For organisations retaining a formal leadership function, it can be challenging to 'let go' of the reins and allow the team to fully self-organise. The coach's role is to help coach the leader and help them transition from a hierarchical leadership model to a distributed leadership model. The role of leaders in the context of self-organising teams therefore changes. In conversation with Colart Miles, an Agile coach and entrepreneur, he explains

> We call it a kind of lean in lean out. When changes like this happen, and they are happening, as a manager, you've got a choice of leaning into the change and or leaning out. And unfortunately, we are hardwired. Our brains are hardwired to keep us all safe. So the first reaction is usually it's a threat. So there's a fear response to them. And that gives rise to a lot of what we see as resistance in the frozen middle layer. And I think they just get a really bad rap. When, if you can overcome that initial shock, from some change happening in your space, and get your bearings and kind of trust that it's coming from a good place. That you have the opportunity and the support to lean into the process, then good things happen. It's a lot like skiing and leaning away from the slope. Which is your natural instinct, right? 'You want me to lean into that!' But when you lean away, you know, your skis lift and crazy stuff. But when you lean in, you have the opportunity to gain more control and influence the way you're actually trying to go.
>
> So that disposition, I think, is incredibly important for our middle management layers. And if they can role model behaviours, what we see is at the squad and team, they will become behaviour amplifiers.

The leader's role changes in a self-organising structure, and the work of the coach can be to help the leader adjust to this change and leverage it as in the previous example. Many organisations moving to Agile ways of working have not prepared for this shift. The organisational implications are understated, and often Agile coaches are left trying to grapple with broader contextual issues before they can start to coach the team. Leading self-organising teams requires a deep appreciation of the organisational landscape and confidence to ride the wave of change. Seeing the leadership role through the lens of functions to be performed can be helpful and provide a signpost for leaders struggling with the new reality. And part of that new reality is the alarming rate at which organisations are adopting Agile practices.

1.5 Coaching Agile and self-organising teams

Coaching Agile teams is a topic on its own, and many great books have been written to support coaching in this specific area. That said, no book on coaching self-organising teams is complete without a conversation on Agile coaching.

Over the years, I've seen and experienced many different forms of Agile coaching depending on the organisation. It seems there are multiple models of applying Agile coaching in practice. There are some common themes and some key differences, which we'll explore for completeness.

There is also a clear distinction between software development-based Agile teams and non-technical Agile teams. For example, Agile H.R. is an emergent area and later in the book we will look at an H.R. team that embraced self-organising teams. I offer the following as an introduction to Agile coaching for those not familiar with it. For those readers who are experts in the field, it might be interesting to see how this squares with your definition of Agile coaching. The following are generalised themes and not attached to any particular framework such as SCRUM or XP.

Domain expertise

Within Agile, the notion of a cross-functional self-organising team is well known. This cross-functional team will likely be biased towards technical challenges in pursuit of product development. To be a successful Agile coach, it's likely that the coach will have some domain expertise. In other words, they will have technical knowledge that they apply to the coaching environment. Jason Little, a well-known Agile coach and Lean Change advocate, explains

> [T]he term coach comes from Extreme Programming in the nineties. That was the first origin of the idea of a coach on a software team. It was all technical in nature. When Agile coaching started to become popular, that's when the door to the greater organisation opened up . . . a good SCRUM master, if they're working with a software team, they should have worked on a software team themselves. . . . if there's a non-technical coach trying to teach me test-driven development by being a coach, that would be very frustrating.

Jason's commentary tells us that the first position of an Agile coach is as a domain expert. In team coaching, the domain expertise is 'teams'. Understanding the context in which you're coaching is essential, but that doesn't mean you need to be a domain expert.

Practices and methods

Tools, methods and practices have increased in the Agile community and the appropriation of organisational development models and techniques in the role of enterprise Agile coaching. Many Agile coaches have a slew of such tools, models and methods at hand and teach the teams Agile practices. This difference between team coaching and Agile team coaching is notable, although not universal. The role of a coach as a teacher is more prevalent in teams that are new to Agile. This teaching role could include techniques for estimating projects as well as lean tools to aid decision making.

In team coaching, we are 'teaching' the team to self-coach. Everything we do within the sessions is with the sole purpose of enabling the team to learn and work together autonomously.

Boundary coordinator

Agile coaches perform a coordinator function similar to one of the leadership functions mentioned earlier. Again, Jason has a great way of describing this:

> For me, the SCRUM masters have always been internally faced towards the team. The agile coach has been more working in the white space, being a bridge and a link between the team and management, the team, the programmes or elsewhere in the organisation.

Team coaches might also perform this function – but it's less likely if your role is as an external coach. This role is challenging because it requires the ability to stay out of the content. There is also a high chance the Agile coach is likely to become invested in the outcome and potentially deprive the team of a learning opportunity.

1.6   Basic principles to get you started

The context for coaching self-organising teams is a rich ground for learning. My first chapter aims to give you just enough to get started and references you can go to for a deeper dive. I would recommend you take one topic to explore in more detail and develop a plan to use what you learn. And that's one of the basic principles we'll cover in this final section.

I offer the following prime directive and basic principles to prompt your thinking and inspire you to explore your own to have a foundation for your team coaching practice.

Prime Directive: leave the team capable of coaching itself

Guiding Principles:

We coach the team in the room and the organisation they represent – individual team members cannot know everything about the organisation. Collectively, the team will have a better understanding of the whole organisation. The parable of the blind men and elephant. Each has a subjective experience of part of the elephant they touch, but none can describe how the whole elephant looks. We are prisoners of our subjective experiences, and only through discussion and exploration can we create an entire picture.

Coach the team on tangible business challenges first – our job is not to 'fix' the team. We assume the team can work effectively on business issues. Our role is to help discover ways of working that increase capability and capacity to improve these skills. In the process, we will help the team work together as a collective whole. They will have the ability to resolve theory issues and come up with solutions through the coaching process.

Focus on creating teaming skills – we coach the team to find better ways of making decisions, navigating conflict, working together and developing resilience to create and join other teams with ease. In the knowledge, they have resources on which to draw.

Assume the team can self-organise – all team members can make decisions and work productively with others given the support and delegated authority. Coach the team to identify their superpowers and help them navigate organisational challenges.

Solutions may not be apparent in only one session – coaching the team to discuss and think through issues might not lead to a ready solution. Sometimes the work happens between the sessions. Support the team in allowing the space for deeper thinking and help co-create processes that support an emergent approach to solution generation.

Deliberate practice requires action and retrospection – Support the team to practice what they are learning. Design into the coaching process the opportunity for the team to gradually assume responsibility for coaching each other. Create opportunities for reflection and insight for further experimentation.

Create a framework for collaboration – teamwork is about interdependence. Co-create how the team will work together and rely on each other collectively to attain their goal. Encourage individual self-discipline in the service of the team. Help the team co-create a powerful shared agenda.

Teams are complex systems, therefore experimentation is essential – there is no magic formula for working with teams. No process can adequately describe how you will work with each team. Whilst there might be some common themes, it is probable that each team will have a different way of combining those themes that creates a unique coaching experience. Tools and techniques are great to have in your toolkit, but the best tool is experimentation and curiosity.

Leave the team in a better place – a second directive of 'first do no harm' guides this final principle. We work with the team to create a supportive and motivating environment that they create for each other. Our goal is to start from where they are and help make it a little better each time we work with the team. We take a solution-focused approach to a future possible state in our coaching stance.

1.7   Chapter summary

I have now set the scene for coaching self-organising teams. This chapter summarises some of the current key research on teams, self-organising, leadership functions and complexity. I offer my summary of the key points at the end of each chapter. I invite you to come up with your summary of the chapter and explore some of the other resources, including further reading and research.

- Complexity and uncertainty create the context for teamwork and why it is becoming increasingly important. Distributed decision making is most helpful in organisations because of dispersed knowledge.
- Teams are different from groups because they have interdependency around task completion and share a common set of objectives to improve performance together.
- Self-organising teams can make decisions, schedule their work, navigate problems, allocate roles and responsibilities and produce results without a formal leadership role.
- The degree to which a team self-organises ranges from self-managing to self-governing. Team selection and responsibility for team performance are two criteria that move the needle from self-managing to self-governing.
- Adopting a self-organising team model requires an organisation to examine its starting point. Purpose and direction need to be clearly aligned with a self-organising model because it challenges hierarchical structures.
- Functional leadership rather than leaders is a better model to follow for a self-organising team. The team can carry out all leadership functions if it is on the self-governing end of the spectrum and most other leadership functions if it is at the self-managed end of the spectrum.

- Agile is not the only environment in which self-organising teams operate. Coaching in Agile has a slightly nuanced approach that distinguishes it from team coaching per se.
- Develop a set of principles for your team coaching practice that consider what we currently know about teams and self-organisation. Be prepared to shift your perspective as your practice develops and new evidence emerges.

Bibliography

Beck, K., et al. (2001) *Agile Manifesto*. http://agilemanifesto.org/. Accessed November 1, 2020.

Edmondson, A. C. (2012) *Teaming: How Organizations Learn, Innovate and Compete in the Knowledge Economy*. San Francisco, CA: John Wiley and Sons.

Edmondson, A. C. (2013) The Three Pillars of a Teaming Culture. *Harvard Business Review* online, December 17, 2013. https://hbr.org/2013/12/the-three-pillars-of-a-teaming-culture. Accessed October 25, 2019.

Edmondson, A. C., and Harvey, J.-F. (2017) *Extreme Teaming: Lessons in Complex, Cross-Sector Leadership*. Bingley, UK: Emerald Publishing Limited.

Hackman, J. R. (1990) *Groups That Work and Those That Don't*. San Francisco, CA: Jossey-Bass.

Hackman, J. R. (2002) *Leading Teams: Setting the Stage for Great Performances*. Boston, MA: Harvard Business School Publishing Corporation.

Hackman, J. R., PhD. (2004) What Makes for a Great Team? *American Psychological Association*. www.apa.org/science/about/psa/2004/06/hackman. Accessed January 25, 2021.

Heylighen, F. (1970) The Science of Self-Organization and Adaptivity, the Science of Self-Organization and Adaptivity. In: *The Encyclopedia of Life Support Systems*, vol. 5.

Hundermark, P., and Kaltenecker, S. (2014) *What Are Self-Organising Teams*. www.infoq.com/articles/what-are-self-organising-teams/.

Ishikawa, K. (1985) *What Is Total Quality Control? The Japanese Way*. Englewood Cliffs, NJ: Prentice Hall.

Kendall, G. (2019) *Apollo 11 Anniversary: Could an iPhone Fly Me to the Moon?* www.independent.co.uk/news/science/apollo-11-moon-landing-mobile-phones-smartphone-iphone-a8988351.html. Accessed November 1, 2020.

Laloux, F. (2014) *Reinventing Organizations*, Illustrated edition. Nelson Parker.

Linders, B. (2016) *Don't Copy the Spotify Model*. www.infoq.com/news/2016/10/no-spotify-model/. Accessed October 29, 2019.

Macy, J., and Brown, M. (2014) *Coming Back to Life*. British Colombia, Canada: New Society Publishers.

Morgeson, F., et al. (2010) Leadership in Teams: A Functional Approach to Understanding Leadership Structures and Processes. *Journal of Management*, vol. 36, no. 1, pp. 5–39. https://doi.org/10.1177/0149206309347376.

Pfeffer, J. (2015) *Leadership BS*. London: Harper Collins.

Revans, R. W. (2011) *ABC of Action Learning*. Farnham, Surrey: Gower Publishing Limited.

Rozovsky, J. (November 17, 2015). *Five Keys to a Successful Google Team*. https://rework.withgoogle.com/blog/five-keys-to-a-successful-google-team/. Accessed January 25, 2021.

Snowden, D. J., and Boone, M. E. (2007) A Leader's Framework for Decision Making. *Harvard Business Review* online. https://hbr.org/2007/11/a-leaders-framework-for-decision-making. Accessed January 25, 2021.

Sutherland, J., and Schwaber, K. (1995) The SCRUM Guide. *Scrum.org*. www.scrumguides.org/scrum-guide.html.

Thomas, L. F., and Harri-Augstein, E. S. (1985) *Self-organised Learning: Foundations of a Conversational Science for Psychology*. London; Boston: Routledge & Kegan Paul.

Wageman, R., Nunes, D. A., Burruss, J. A., and Hackman, J. R. (2008) *Senior Leadership Teams*. Boston, MA: Harvard Business School Press.

Chapter 2

How to set up for progress and success

Coaching starts from the moment you talk with a potential client or team. How well the relationship works depends on many factors. This chapter explores some of the core elements of creating the bedrock for healthy and productive coaching conversations.

The first part of this chapter talks about the cornerstone of setting up teams for success – the coaching system, the organisational context, agreeing on some foundational rules and creating a climate of psychological safety. Often when working with teams on the dysfunctional end of the spectrum, there are undeclared assumptions and hidden agendas either at a team level or at an organisational level. One essential activity for the coach is to create transparency by declaring expectations and understanding who is commissioning the team and the context in which the team is working.

Of equal importance as knowing when to coach a team is to know when to step away. Dysfunction per se is an indicator of deeper-rooted underlying issues. However, it does not necessarily mean that the team is uncoachable. If there is an unwillingness to work with the coaching process and no desire to change, that is the time to realise coaching might not be the best approach for the team. Organisations sometimes pursue team development in the face of contradictory evidence that either the team is a group or, on the other hand, the team has reached a natural point where disbandment is the best choice.

Trust – this word crops up regularly when talking to people about working in teams. It turns out we should be talking about psychological safety rather than trust as it is a better fit. According to Amy Edmondson (1999), trust exists in the individual's mind about a 'target individual or organisation' – we cannot develop trust with a 'group' of people. The reason is that trust is more about the individual's perceived expectation of how people are likely to act with us on an individual basis. One coach asked me how they could create trust when their natural personality is introverted. This definition of trust probably helps coaches with similar questions. We develop trust one on one with team members. The discovery process that we'll explore in more detail is an ideal opportunity to create trust. During our one-to-one sessions with team members, we can get to know them better, and they can get to know us. Edmondson isn't saying that trust isn't essential. She is

DOI: 10.4324/9781003110583-3

merely saying that trust is what we have with one another. At a team level, it's psychological safety that's important. So, it would be best if you had both, but they are different.

We cannot know how a group will behave with us, only an individual within the team, based on our learned experience of them. Edmondson goes onto explain that we can have trust in a company through their brand. In other words, brands create customer trust. Teams, on the other hand, do not have a brand. It is difficult to predict how a group of people will act because it is a complex system made up of individuals. We may well have trust with one or two individuals based on our experience, but we still cannot know how the team will act. Psychological safety over trust is what we should consider in teams.

2.1   Contracting and psychological safety

Many organisations approach initiatives with enthusiasm, spending little time thinking about how people will work together in practice and how this might impact or be impacted by the organisation system in which they operate. Before we enter the realm of the team, we must first understand what's happening within the organisation. In a complex world, we cannot rely on a simple linear process to help us with this challenging task. Instead, we must think of it as an interrelated system that helps create or detract from creating an environment or climate of psychological safety. In the following diagram, I attempt to represent this to demonstrate some of the activities to consider when establishing teams and, more importantly, self-organising teams.

When we are in the domain of complexity, self-organisation requires us to take a different approach to how we introduce an idea into an organisation.

In my initial ideas for this chapter, in my mind, I automatically created a linear process. Thinking back to the conversation earlier about complexity, I realised I had fallen into the same trap as many organisations. Contracting is one of the areas that require more detailed exploration. The word contracting is a legal-sounding word. The reality is about agreeing on how the team coaching will operate and how the organisational system will work with the team. It covers both the What and the How. More will be discussed later on in this chapter.

I have attempted to demonstrate some critical areas for consideration when introducing a team-based approach to self-organising teamwork. On the one hand, you could draw this as a linear model and an iterative linked cycle. It suggests to me on further investigation that the activities outlined are connected and have potential knock-on. For example, in preparing teams for success, an organisation is continually preparing and reviewing. In the preparation phase, you are looking at what the organisation is seeking to achieve through teams. There will be a task the organisation is asking the team to perform, and this task must fit within the broader context of the organisation. One of the things I've learned about complexity is rather than having a goal, far better to have a destination in which the organisation is heading. This destination over an endpoint allows the organisation

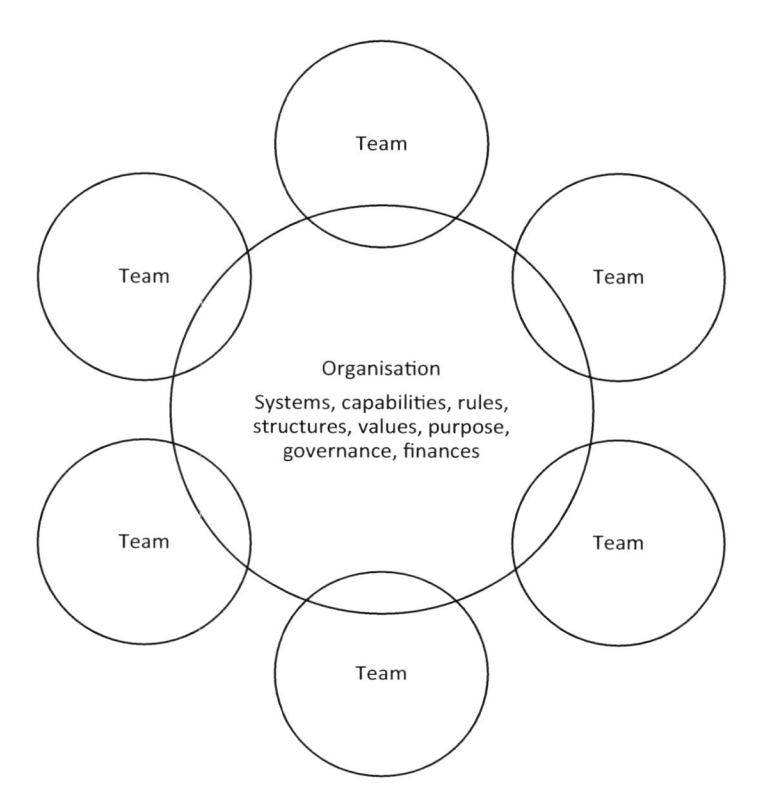

Enabling Constraints – Topics for consideration
- Team selection e.g. hiring and firing
- Work task allocation
- Client relationships e.g. seeking, serving, growing
- Remuneration and recognition
- Performance standards – setting, monitoring, correcting
- Scope and reach – setting, reviewing, extending or reducing

Figure 2.1 Creating a Self-Organising System

to take advantage of opportunities that occur. For example, no one could have predicted the COVID-19 pandemic in 2020. Plans organisations had in place had to be changed entirely. Therefore, preparing and planning must be sufficiently flexible to allow for changes in the environment, employees, customer requirements, etc. Preparing is not an end. It is an iterative activity that includes preparing the teams for change, review and updating.

Commissioning the team

Commissioning is the green light for the team to start work. It is also the delegated authority for the scope and decision making for the team. For example, teams need to understand what they are required to achieve in terms of the deliverables. The organisation needs to have clear ideas on this. Hackman (1990) discusses some of the reasons groups don't work well.

The case studies cited demonstrate how teams with no clue about what they are doing or why often fall into disrepair. This lack of direction can create an assumption that the team is dysfunctional; this leads to the view that the team is at fault, whereas the root cause lies in poorly defined objectives and purpose. The reality is, without a clear understanding of what the team is expected to achieve, the team will never succeed. One team I worked with was tasked with developing an improvement idea that could save the organisation money. The team worked over several weeks, engaging with the senior leadership and finally presented their idea with the related savings. The senior leadership team rejected the idea. With hindsight, the commissioning phase of the project was severely limited. The goal of saving money was clear, and the team felt they had been given delegated authority to achieve the task, but the scope and boundaries were not explicit. The team was demoralised and felt undervalued by the end of the process.

Commissioning isn't a one-time effect. It's something that you do and review based on data that are coming into the organisation system. For example, the team may not have all the data at its fingertips that someone at a higher level in the organisation might have; therefore, someone needs to ensure that the team can access that information. In effect, you are constantly commissioning and re-commissioning the team as new data become available, albeit in small doses.

Scoping

Setting the ground rules for what the team can and cannot do within the bounds of organisational requirements means that the team can have some level of certainty about what deliverables are expected. The scope needs to be sufficiently clear, and the boundaries of the work defined to enable the team to estimate, plan and develop the outcome. The team needs to be appraised of any scope changes, including why they are happening. Scope change also requires a review of skills and capabilities. Does the team have the necessary resources in place to deliver the updated scope? The scope should also consider the organisation's capacity, including existing workload and projects.

The overall aim of coaching is to enable the team to self-coach. During the coaching process, the coach passes on knowledge and transitions the team to become capable of self-coaching and coach other teams to create a living system of self-organising teams. For an external coach, this can present an interesting paradox. In helping the team self-coach, the external coach is no longer required, impacting the coach's revenue opportunity. However, this also offers an opportunity for the external coach to develop another revenue stream – helping coach other coaches within the organisation and therefore, creating coaching capability for the organisation to become self-sustaining. Buurtzorg, a company we will become very familiar with by the end of this book, has a regional coach resource pool.

In some of the organisations I interviewed, people could work in more than one team. Working in multiple teams requires even greater teaming skills. There is an opportunity for a transitioning process to enable them to move seamlessly between teams. The role of the coach becomes an enabler of self-organising as a natural process. If a natural process is an aim, it makes it even more important to create a climate for psychological safety.

Agreeing

Contracting is another name for how the team will interact with each other, the coach, the broader organisation and its stakeholders, and updating progress. There are many different scenarios for coaches in organisations as it becomes part of the organisational, operational model. These scenarios include:

- Team leader as coach
- Manager as coach
- Internal coach as part of a coaching pool
- External team coach
- Informal internal coach

Depending on your role and the type of organisation you are working with, as an external coach, you might be engaged at different stages in the coaching cycle:

- Coaching the team leader
- Coaching the team as it forms
- Coaching the team through a specific challenge
- Coaching the team to transition to self-coaching

Contracting is the process of creating an agreement. Contracting is a coaching specific term concerning how the team will work together and what the team will be working on. This agreement process happens at the beginning of the coaching relationship. In the beginning, you discuss how you will work together as a team and the context for the coaching. It can also happen within the coaching sessions themselves concerning the task or topic for the session and how you will work together in that specific session.

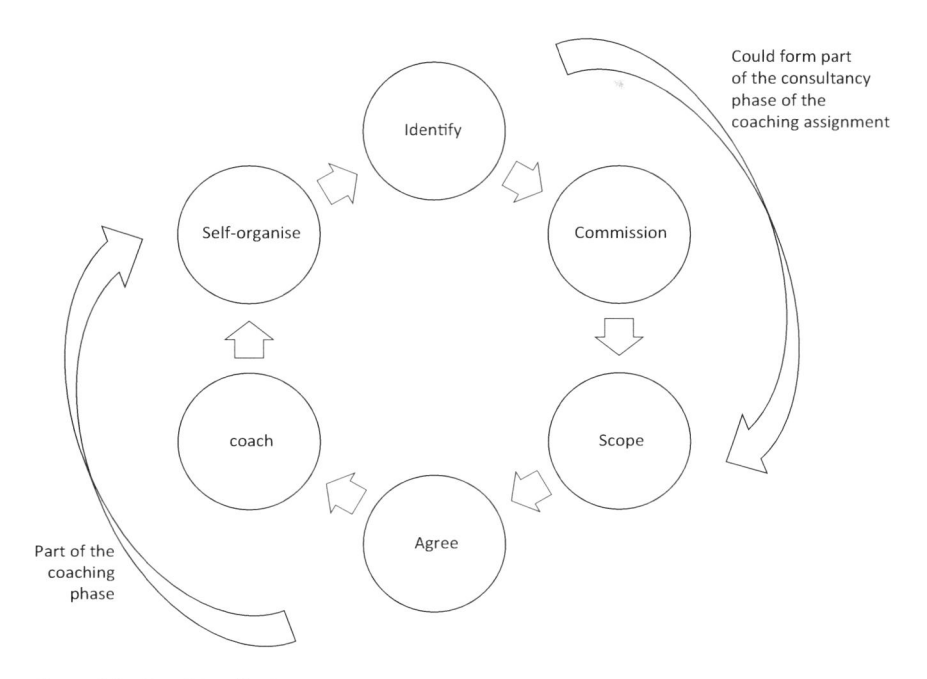

Could form part of the consultancy phase of the coaching assignment

Part of the coaching phase

Figure 2.2 Coaching Cycle

Contracting is not a one-time event. As a coach, you are constantly contracting and re-contracting during the coaching relationship. Each time you meet with the team, you are re-contracting. Even within the session itself, you are re-contracting with the team, mainly if you're doing something outside of the agreed agenda for the coaching session. You might be asking questions such as 'How does what we're discussing now match what we agreed? Would you like to spend more time on this topic or move on?' In effect, you are using observation and insight to test what the team wants from you and the coaching conversation. The contracting process is one of the enablers of psychological safety allowing the team to surface undeclared assumptions and explore what it is they wish to do next and what direction the coaching conversation takes.

In interviewing other coaches and experts for this book, I noticed different kinds of coaching approaches depending on the skills of the coach and the context in which they are coaching. In the social care sector, Yumi Stamet explained that the coach might well be an internal coach who has previously carried out a team leader role with that team, therefore, knows the content on which the team is working. It could be that the team is looking for advice and guidance from the coach on how the team tackles a specific content-related activity. In other words, they need clear input on what to do next because they don't have either the experience or the expertise; as Stamet says, 'They might never had to use any of the systems, like, for example, their client relationship management systems, CRMS. Now they have to because they're the ones that are actually recording what is being done with clients'. In this scenario, the coach will play more of a mentoring role. They are sharing their knowledge with the team so that they can carry out this function in the future.

We will look at Buurtzorg, another organisation in the healthcare sector that uses regional coaches to help teams do precisely this kind of thing. If we take a pure coaching stance and not share our knowledge, this can be frustrating for both individuals and teams who just want to know the answer. In traditional coaching, we are often taught not to give advice and guidance and give answers. Therefore, it relies on the coach's skills to help guide the team without being overly directive in terms of what to do. For example, that might mean giving third-party stories 'Would it be helpful for me to tell you about what happened when I did this in the past? I will then ask you your thoughts on the story, and what insights you've got and how that might help you or not carry out the task you're struggling with'. This tangential approach is one way of helping the team without going into the stereotypical coach mode of asking a question on a question. Sometimes a story that helps illustrates a potential path triggers the team's idea generation. The key is that as the coach, you don't become attached to your own story and overly push the answer to the team. If, however, you are operating from a position of knowledge and know for sure that if the team takes a particular course of action, it could have dire consequences, you have an ethical duty to share.

The coach's goal is to help the team understand and find their way to move forward. This approach demonstrates how you move from coaching into a mentoring role. If you are a subject matter expertise, it becomes a resource for the team to use or not as they choose. Contracting with the team first before you do this is part of establishing the agreements on how you will work together.

Yumi Stamet offers her thoughts on what happens in the early days of team formation. It is often this kind of help that the team is looking for, particularly when they are new to working together as a team and, more importantly, as a self-organising team. Stamet points out, 'We're actually helping the team to self-organise elements of the job they've never done before'. If you are coaching a team without that content expertise, then you might address this challenge by asking the team to think about who they might speak with, where they might go to for resources and helping them create a plan of how they will get that information.

The previous point demonstrates how team coaching is not as straightforward as individual coaching. As a team coach, your role is to provide more than just reflection space and powerful questioning – your role is to help the team learn and work out things for themselves. It could be that, in a session, no solution is apparent. Only through further reflection, investigation and working together outside of the session will the team find some resolution. Helping the team realise that this is as powerful as focusing on solutions per se enables the team to become self-organising. As part of how team coaching works, declaring this upfront is part of the agreement framing and the lifeblood of contracting.

There are many different ways of creating coaching agreements. The chapter on tools goes into some of these later in the book. One approach that worked well with one team was individual meetings with team members as part of the discovery process, including the team leader, to ascertain what they were looking for working together as a team. These one-on-one sessions included finding out:

- What outcomes they wanted
- What success meant for them working together as a team
- What behaviours they wanted to see
- What behaviours they didn't want to see
- What they were expecting from me as the coach
- What I was expecting from them as a team.

In our first team session, I talked them through what they'd asked for during the interviews. I collated all the information together and presented it back to them. I then did an activity to cement what we needed from each other and called it 'Putting Your Cards on the Table'.

I took a pack of playing cards and placed blank stickers on one side of the card and wrote down some of the things I was expecting from the team. I put these cards on the table, discussing each one individually. I handed out three playing cards with blank stickers to everyone and asked them to write on the cards what they wanted from the team and me. We collated all the cards together and created themes. We had our cards on the table before starting to work together. That worked well, and during the break, one of the team members came up to me, taking me to one side and said that they were happy we had done the activity as they were fearful a specific member of the team might take over and talk too much during the sessions. The cards activity enabled the team to have a conversation together in the open in a safe way before we got into the session itself. It also helped the team self-regulate the amount of airtime each person had during conversations. As the coach, it also helped me understand my role in assisting the team to surface challenges around how they worked together. Be explicit about your role as the coach. It enables the team to self-coach, brings out into the open boundaries and co-creates an environment for mutual exploration.

When coaching teams, you often find that you have individuals coming up to you to give insights about how they're feeling about the team. Sometimes it's pretty challenging to deal with those outside the agreement you've made with the team. One way that I handle this is to ask the individual, 'How comfortable are you talking about that within the team?' If they are, we create some space to introduce the topic after the break and introduce the conversation. If they aren't, I ask coaching questions to enable some level of deeper understanding about what's going on for them, the team and the broader system acting as interference. Questions such as

- What's getting in the way of sharing this with the team?
- How else might we address the situation?
- How might sharing this become a resource for the team?
- How might this become a learning point for the team?
- What might the team miss out on by not sharing this?
- What implications are there for you personally in sharing this information with the team?

The responsibility for sorting and resolving issues is passed to the team itself rather than the coach as the conduit. It's like a relay race where the individual passes the baton to you as the coach, and you pass the baton back to the individual who passes it on to the team to resolve their dilemma. Understanding where the boundaries lie between you as the coach and you as the quasi-leader of the team forms part of the contracting phase. As a coach, we never want to become the leader of the team. If you find yourself in that position, it's an indication you must re-establish the contract with the team. In team coaching, everyone, including the coach, is an equal party in the activities and coaching process. The tools in Chapter 5 go into more detail on the contracting process. Hopefully, this vignette has illustrated some of the challenges around boundaries between the coach and the team itself.

Creating psychological safety is one of the goals of the contracting process. Amy Edmondson poses some great questions in her book The Fearless Organisation, which are now in the public domain, and these are also in Chapter 5 of this book. The questions are a great litmus test for how people are feeling within the team. An approach for using these questions could be to use them at intervals during your coaching assignment with the team. For example, midway point or quarterly ask the team questions relating to psychological safety.

One team I worked with had a very combative and robust approach to discussing issues. From outside the team, this sounded like a descent into conflict. I waited and watched what the team was doing and, after a while, decided to intervene. The intervention I took was to give an observation and ask a question: 'I'm sensing that there's some frustration within the team. Would you like some help?' The team's response was, 'No, go away. We're resolving it and will let you know when we need your help'. They battled through the issue and a few minutes later said, 'Now we need your help'. Asking a question based on what I was hearing and sensing, let the team know I was aware and ready to help. I let the team choose if or when they wanted that help.

It's too easy to step in and rescue the team when we see it struggling. Not only can this be disempowering, but it also helps create a dependency on you as the coach to 'rescue' the team when it runs into difficulties. As a coach, you need to listen and sense whether the team feels safe to have robust conversations, known as radical candour, and trust the team will know when they've reached a sticking point. Being able to speak freely is essential and an indicator of psychological safety. Edmondson's questions help pinpoint specific issues, but you're always listening for how the group works together as the coach. Looking for signs they can resolve their issues, they are on task and the conversation is adding to or detracting from completion of the task and sense when they have gone off track and helping them get back on track.

Contracting and psychological safety are two linchpins for effective team working. The team's ability to create its contract and establish and maintain safety within that space of working together is perhaps one of the critical skills a self-organising team can acquire. As teams move towards self-organisation and maturity, having an honest and open conversation, checking in that the team is on track and working together, you can introduce other aspects of self-organisation as the team matures.

Managing the team's and individuals' performance challenges teams the most, particularly if one or two team members are not pulling their weight or under-performing on tasks. The ability to coach each other and have a supportive and open conversation is next-level self-organisation. Laurent Prodon, an Agile coach working in an organisation following a holacratic model, reflected on this question, 'So you are really 100% responsible for the success of your circle. One of the big challenges that comes in parallel to this is the feedback culture . . . try to make sure that people know how to give feedback. So we have feedback training, for example, and also know how to receive feedback, which is also very important'. Naturally, this approach also applies to how the organisation interacts with the teams. The holacratic model is very prescriptive on roles and responsibilities within the circles (teams) and meeting cycles. Prodon's reflection underpins the importance of training team members in critical processes that support self-organisation. In this case, it relates to feedback: how the organisation makes it part of 'how we work together'. Contracting between the organisation and the team itself needs to be as robust as between the team and the coach. Organisations moving towards a self-organising team model must consider what kind of relationship they want with the teams and how they will ensure a psychologically safe space for the teams to own the work they've been tasked to do. This will necessarily mean looking at delegated authority, role and responsibility, boundary management and how the team will generally operate within the bounds of corporate governance.

Identifying the team and reason for coaching

Coaching self-organising teams isn't just about the process of coaching the team. There is much work upfront in establishing who the team is and why coaching is considered the appropriate intervention. As you will see from what we've discussed earlier, commissioning the team is the most critical indicator of success. The organisation identifies what needs to be done, the overall destination in terms of its goals, where it is now and what needs improving or changing. Clarity on this enables the right resource – financial, people, and technical – to be allocated to address the challenge that lies ahead.

In my research, I found that skills are an important part; however, they are not the only determinant of successful teams. In their research Project Aristotle, Google found that the key factor of success was psychological safety. The skills of the team, whilst important we're not the thing that determines success overall. If the organisation is asking a team to look at a technical deliverable, as in Agile teams, there needs to be technical expertise within the team to deliver that result. As we know, teams also need to be sufficiently diverse to enable innovation and creativity. Research also suggests that having a cross-functional team allows learning and informs a much wider solution to the challenge. Selecting the right team is not as simple as looking at what resources you have available. It's a combination of skills, talents, capacity and capability, as well as that special ingredient of attitude and personal attributes. Diverse teams provide a rich and fertile ground in which teams can succeed. There is evidence suggesting that too diverse in certain circumstances is not a good thing. Cases in which diversity plays to a team's strength include working on a shared task.

There is also contrary research that suggests that where diversity around functional backgrounds exists in a team, even with a shared task, this can sometimes be a source of task conflict (Pelled et al. 1999). We might not always have the luxury of being part of the commissioning phase. We can ask questions about the team member selection process to appreciate what context we'll be entering when we coach the team. In some organisations, teams can self-select. This adds a further dimension of complexity. Notwithstanding likely bias in self-selecting, it might mean that the team is either too homogenous or too diverse. A valuable resource for equipping yourself with more background on self-selecting teams is found in Mamoli and Mole (2015).

As coaches, we need to be clear on answering the question, 'Why coaching?' Our role as coaches is to help organisations understand the ingredients of productive teams. Is coaching the most appropriate intervention? If the goal is to equip the team to self-coach and become self-sustaining, coaching is the likely answer.

Any book on coaching would not be complete without a comparison between the different types of intervention. In the 15 or so years I have been formally coaching, this is one of the areas I have iterated many times. In Gorell (2013), I offer some thoughts on the difference between coaching, mentoring and counselling. To assist you in helping understand which hat you're wearing, I provide some guidance in the following table.

Coaching teams probably requires us to swing between all roles but primarily stay in the coaching arena most times. For example, our early conversations with stakeholders and team members will naturally lend themselves to a consulting stance. As team coaches, we need to be transparent with ourselves about the hat we're wearing and ensure we have clear boundaries between each. Knowing when to offer a process to facilitate conversation over creating a space for the team to discover is one such boundary.

Table 2.1 Clarifying the Coach's Role

Coach	Facilitator	Trainer	Mentor	Consultant
Intervention style				
How is not having this expertise affecting you as a team? What do you collectively want to do about that?	Who will speak first? Let's go round the room individually to hear everyone's thoughts	What skills so you need as a team? What is the gap? Here's how we might fill that gap	Here's what I experienced in a team that worked well	Here's a tool to help diagnose what's missing in the team I've analysed the outputs – these are my recommendations

Using different approaches

At the beginning of the coaching phase, the emphasis is typically on helping the team establish the contract or agreement. How the team will work together, helping create a climate for learning. The approach here might have a more substantial facilitation element.

For a team that's been around for a long time and is slightly more mature, it might be about how they move from getting stuck. Maybe they've fallen into some dysfunction, and things aren't working as well. There might some conflict. Coaching here is about helping them learn how to work through conflict and make it positive and creative and understand how they can learn together to coach themselves. It might also include how to do peer-to-peer coaching, for example, or how to give and receive feedback. The approach here is more likely to be in the coaching arena, helping create a space for the team to co-explore without expectation.

If we return to Morgesen et al. (2010), the two distinct phases for teams help us pinpoint where the team is in their cycle and how coaching might help: the setup phase or the action phase. Morgesen et al.'s model is a great starting point to identify which stance you might take and which tools to use. Consider how you might make this model a tool to use in your practice and guide which hat to put on. Take a moment to reflect on what you have done in the past. Bringing this into your conscious awareness means you can wear hats with purpose rather than falling into behaviour patterns that don't help you or support the team.

2.2   Setting up a learning mindset

The core learning aim of self-organising teams is:

> To work autonomously so that the team can manage everyday task and resolve dilemmas for itself.

The coach aims to help the team develop this self-sufficiency. To do this, a team needs practice in co-creation, co-determination and the ability to learn and improve. We all have different experiences of learning at school – some positive, some not so positive. How we experienced learning in our childhood will influence our attitudes to learning in adulthood. My business partner and I worked with a team and were puzzled by how they responded to learning opportunities. The discussions were slow to take off, and no one wanted to make the first comment. Through exploring what was happening and the use of humour, we had our answer. We realised that there were many type-A personalities, as they described it, in the team who did not want to get the answer 'wrong'. We discussed the implications of this on their learning, and after encouragement, more discussion, a willingness to engage in free-flow sharing emerged. Our mindset about learning shapes how we adapt to challenges and setbacks and is an essential resource for teams to explore. Working together in a complex environment means that things will not always go according to plan. How the team addresses this when it happens sets the scene for healthy or dysfunctional conflict. Fear of getting something wrong will stint a team's growth unless they find tactics for dealing with this all-too-common thinking. After all, we are taught in school to pass exams, and it is hard to re-wire our thinking when presented with another possibility. A team's ability to learn will determine how readily they adjust to self-organising and develop resilience when faced with setbacks.

BJ Fogg (2020) describes learning as 'the process by which your brain facilitates a change in behaviour in response to your environment'. Dehaene (2020) offers further guidance on the process of learning, embedded in what he describes as the four pillars, the 'secret ingredients of successful learning':

- What we pay attention to
- Our curiosity
- Our ability to correct errors
- The brain's ability to consolidate learning through sleep

Dehaene's book on learning demonstrates the importance of making this topic front and centre for all team coaching. There is a concept within Zen Buddhism called Shoshin – the beginner's mind. By allowing the mind to be curious and open regardless of the level of expertise. Curiosity relates to one of the four pillars outlined by Dehaene, which he characterises as the brain's ability to create endless hypotheses for testing. Hypothesis creation and testing is an excellent analogy for coaching. Since we are walking along the same path as the team, openly engaging in possibility and testing out ideas with detachment, this way of thinking is fundamental to helping a team learn together.

Engaging with teams early in the coaching process means establishing the mindset each member has concerning learning and working with the team to develop a shared mental model of what a learning mindset means for the team. And how this shared mental model will be affected by and impact other stakeholders. For instance, an experimental approach might work well in the team but could trigger a risk response from leaders in the organisation. How will the team fit its learning model into the context of the broader organisation? Should it fit? I offer the following questions as a starter conversation:

- What might it mean for us as a team in how we think about challenges, possibility, setbacks and opportunities?
- What opinions do we each hold about learning?
- Where does that opinion come from?
- What attitudes do we want to foster to help create a learning environment?
- What does a learning environment look, sound and feel like for us?
- How will we measure our learning success?

No discussion on learning mindset can be complete without mentioning the important work of Carol Dweck (2008), who herself opened the possibility of learning differently. Her important research around mindset identifies two types of mindsets that impact our ability to learn: fixed and growth. The fixed mindset sees everything as laid down. We have a requisite level of IQ and talent, and our success or failure depends on this pre-determined level of ability. On the other hand, the growth mindset suggests that we can continually improve and see learning to extend our ability. There may well be a pass or fail in both scenarios, but how we approach 'failure' determines our success. If we see it as an opportunity to learn even more, we can always re-do the 'test'. The concept of 'not yet' is paramount in a growth mindset. We may never become world-class, but we can always improve against our performance. See Chapter 7 for more on this.

The concept of a growth mindset for teams is becoming more important in a virtually connected world. Organisations that pit teams against each other are creating and buying into a zero-sum view of performance. That one team succeeds at the expense of another. In a collaborative world, using the concept of growth mindset, the team's performance is referenced against its previous best. All teams improve and create a network of autonomous teams designed for collaboration, not competition. That is not to say healthy competition isn't good too – the emphasis is the key. If organisations focus too much on competition, it will be challenging to create a curious and open system. Self-organisation that is based on competition might produce high levels of destructive conflict consequently or as a side effect.

The ability to correct errors is embedded in the growth mindset. Stanislas' pillar on our ability to correct errors is an important way of thinking for the team to improve performance together as a team. Errors are gaps in what we expect to what we actually get.

One tool that helps with the ability to correct 'errors' is the retrospective. An important point to note is the interval between the activity and the retrospective. The feedback loop needs to be sufficiently salient for learning to take place. Therefore, a retrospective at the end of the year will not be helpful in the learning process. In team coaching terms, a retrospective each time the team meets is likely to help the team learn quicker and help embed the learning. Repetition is part of the learning process, and retrospectives provide a deliberate practice around error correction and repetition.

There are hundreds of ways to run retrospective conversations. There are some examples in Chapter 5. The key areas investigated in a retrospective are:

- Review what happened, what was expected to happen and understand what went well and how this might be leveraged or replicated
- Review what didn't go so well and what was unexpected and understand what made it so and what else could be done next time
- Identify ideas or opportunities that emerged from the learning

We will return to the topic of retrospectives in more detail in Chapter 7.

Hopefully, it is apparent that contracting, psychological safety and learning mindset form a firm foundation on which the team and the coaches working with the team help create an environment in which the team can progress. I purposely avoid the word succeed, because if we apply a growth mindset, we know that success is about progress. That said, the team should also have clear outcomes in mind and understand where they are heading. Keeping an open mind about what is possible and enabling the team to adapt set up the team to work together in the long term.

2.3   Creating predictability and certainty – boundaries and scoping

The final piece of the puzzle relates more to the coach or coaches than the team per se. This puzzle piece is about understanding what the coach is there to do and managing their scope and boundaries.

A troubling trend among some Agile Coaches suggests that boundary management is one of the areas that need particular attention. A recent tweet suggested that an Agile coach felt that their role was to help teams who were suffering. The implication was that this suffering could impact their family and economic stability entwined with work. A desire to help end a team's suffering on the surface seems laudable and comes from a position of wanting to help. Let's remind ourselves of one of our core principles in coaching teams: Coach the team on tangible business challenges first. It is not our job to fix the team. We must guard against going outside the boundaries of our role. Unless we are qualified therapists or financial advisers, we should 'stick to the knitting'. The coach in the tweet example might have had expertise in therapeutic models, but unless this is the case, it is always advisable to stick to coaching on real business issues. Our role as a coach is not an expert on the content. We are experts in team coaching techniques, tools and methods. Getting clear on your boundaries, the scope of work you are there to do with the team is vital for the coach as it is for the team. Boundary management is especially challenging for team leaders transitioning to the role of team coach.

Stamet explained some of the operational challenges in transitioning team leaders' experiences where the team leader, now coach, is still officially the person allocated for authorising leave, shifts swap and payroll. Setting out clear boundaries helps create a safety net for the coach and a map for the team. In this scenario, the coach could agree on a time frame over which they will train the team to handle these issues for themselves. In fully self-organising teams, incorporate these hygiene roles in the team, so each team member is responsible either full-time or on a rotating basis to perform these tasks. Creating a simple RACI matrix to help clarify roles and responsibilities during the transition phase helps. RACI Stands for Responsible, Accountable, Consulted, Informed. I have used this model many times in process improvement and project work. It is often useful when teams get stuck because no one knows what they are meant to be doing. It gives clarity and creates a conversation from which understanding emerges. Once complete, it also provides a visual cue if placed on a wall, so that team members can refer to it as needed. The definitions are:

- Responsible: does the work to complete the activity
- Accountable: ultimately accountable for the outcome of the team. They are also responsible for delegating the work task, assigning resources and reviewing the outcomes. This person is usually the key sponsor or leader of the team
- Consulted: provides input on the work, particularly regarding how it will impact their future work or domain of expertise
- Informed: kept in the loop on progress

Here's a simple RACI matrix at Table 2.2 for the example quoted earlier. Naturally, who does what will depend on the level of autonomy and delegated authority given to the team. A new RACI model is created each time authority changes within the team and interacts with the organisation. Chapter 5 covers more on how to use the RACI tool.

It is crucial to craft a meaningful contract with the team on what you expect from the team and where you draw your line in the sand. For example, I co-coached a team that was very loose with its interpretation of 'time commitment'. Team members were constantly flitting in and out of the sessions, and when something 'more important' came up, they would leave the session. The re-prioritising of other work during a session seemed to be the cultural norm. Challenging this behaviour was both confronting and surprising. With hindsight, having a more explicit boundary on what, we the coaches, would do if we felt the commitment to the time was lacking would have helped set clear expectations. So, it's not just enough to have a ground rule. It's also important to know what you will do if that ground rule is transgressed.

In Gorell (2013), I discuss the difference between content and process and directive versus non-directive coaching figure 2.3 is a simple tool you can use to work out where you will feel comfortable.

Table 2.2 RACI Example

RACI During Team Set-Up Phase

Activity	Roles			
	Team Sponsor	Team/Project Lead*	Team Member	Coaches*
Payroll	I	R		R
Annual leave	I	R	C	R
Shift swaps	I	R	C	R

RACI During Action Phase

Activity	Roles			
	Team Sponsor	Team/Project Lead*	Team Member	Coaches*
Payroll	C	N/A	R	N/A
Annual leave	I	N/A	R	N/A
Shift swaps	I	N/A	R	N/A

*These roles might be the same person if the team or project leader is transitioning to a team coaching role

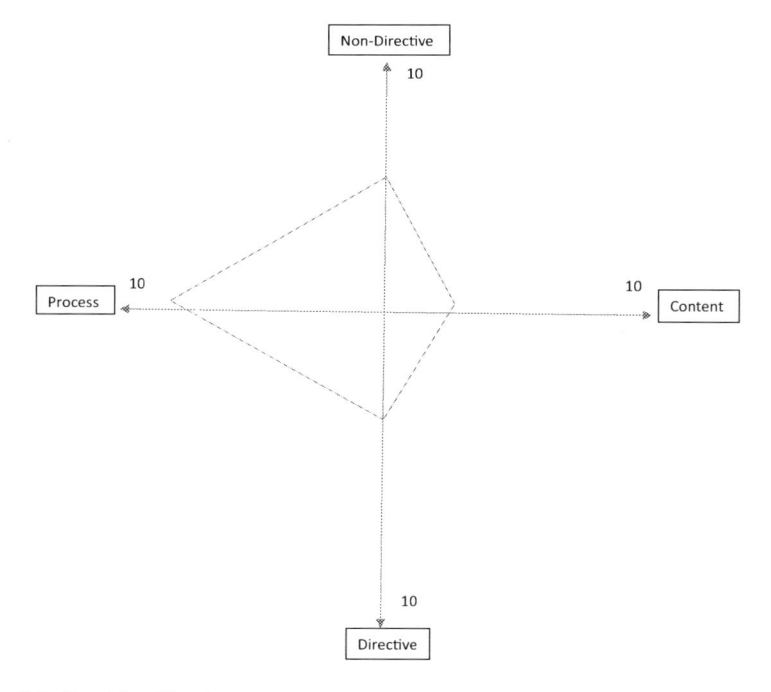

Figure 2.3 Coaching Continua

Source: Copyright Gorell, R (2013). Reproduced with permission from Kogan Page Ltd

Typically working with teams does require a more directive approach than one-on-one coaching. Providing observation and tools to help the team is a directive intervention. Let us return to the situation at the beginning of this section where the Agile coach was hoping to help teams who are suffering. We can use the lens of content over process: the coach is likely to become personally interested in the detail of the team's issues which might lead to attachment to the outcome. They become too invested in the team's situation. It is also likely that they would offer advice and guidance on what the team should do.

Similarly, they are likely to be stepping into the directive zone by 'deciding' for the team how they might address their' suffering'. That's before we start to investigate the notion of 'suffering' and who decides what this is. The Agile coach has already made some assumptions and judgements about what 'suffering' means for the team. All of this is in the context of the coach operating from a position of helping – sometimes, when coaching teams, we have to intuit when we have moved from helper to rescuer.

When we care too much about the outcome for our clients, we can sometimes disempower them to make their own choices and seek their solutions. In that sense, we become expert on their problem. We create a dynamic for the coaching because the team continues to look to the coach for solutions. The team should learn how to resolve dilemmas. In this regard, we will have reduced our effectiveness as a coach and undermined the goal of team coaching to help teams become autonomous and solution-capable.

Creating certainty for the teams, we coach what they can expect from us and what we can expect from them sets the relationship on the right path. That's not to say there won't be diversions along the way. The contracting, boundary and scope setting process helps create safety for the team to explore and navigate when it finds itself lost. The following simple activity helps you and the team work out

Table 2.3 Identifying Boundaries and Scope Activity

Role	Purpose	Boundary	Scope in/out
Coach/es	To help the team become self-sufficient in managing tasks and resolving dilemmas	For example, what role the coach plays within the team	
Team leader/ manager	To provide direction and scope	For example, who decides what the team is there to do and who is included in the team?	
Team members	To work collaboratively with other team members	For example, what's acceptable and not acceptable within the team	
Stakeholder	To provide context for the team's work tasks	For example, will they be invited in to team meetings?	

where boundaries of 'helping' lie and creates an opportunity for conversation. If you are co-coaching the team, both coaches can do a simple activity before coaching together. You can add to it as the conversation evolves and use it to work out loud as you discuss the potential sticking points.

In a later chapter, we will explore one of the ways teams navigate relationships and problem-solving. Having a clear map set up at the beginning is one of the foundation stones for creating constructive conflict that fosters creativity and collaboration whilst recognising our human traits.

2.4   Chapter summary

- Helping create psychological safety is essential for team effectiveness. Establishing trust between individuals is part of the coaching system.
- Contracting is about how you will work together with the team and what the coaching is about. It is a two-way process.
- Self-organising teamwork doesn't follow a linear path. It is more of an iterative and interlinked evolution.
- Commissioning teams means setting a framework in which they can make decisions and become self-sustaining.
- Scoping the work to be done is essential if the team is to have a clear mandate.
- Use the discovery phase of coaching to help establish some of the agreements you'll co-create with the team.
- Creating a climate where teams can speak freely and have a robust conversation is a hallmark of psychological safety.
- Creating a system for giving and receiving feedback is essential if teams are to improve performance together.
- Selecting team members is a nuanced activity even where they self-select. Too much diversity can be as challenging as too little. Thought and care are required before teams are commissioned.
- Coaching is one of many different kinds of interventions. Be clear about which hat you're wearing, and stay on the coaching side of the fence most of the time.
- A team's ability to learn will determine how readily they adjust to self-organising and develop resilience when faced with setbacks.
- Know what action is required when a ground rule is transgressed. Learning together with the team about boundary management is a key facet of collaboration.
- We help co-create an environment where the team can resolve its dilemmas. Our role is to help, not rescue the team.

Bibliography

Appello, J. (2011) *Management 3.0: Leading Agile Developers, Developing Agile Leaders*. Addison-Wesley Professional.

Dehaene, S. (2020) *How We Learn*. New York, NY: Penguin Random House.

Dweck, C. S. (2008) *Mindset the New Psychology of Success*. New York, NY: Ballantine Books.

Edmondson, A. (1999) *The Fearless Organization*. Hoboken, NJ: Wiley.

Fogg, B. J. (2020) *Tiny Habits*. Boston, UK: Houghton Mifflim Harcourt.

Gorell, R. (2013) *Group Coaching*, London, UK: Kogan Page.

Hackman, J. R. (1990) *Groups That Work and Those That Don't*. San Francisco, CA: Jossey-Bass.

Mamoli, S., and Mole, D. (2015) *Creating Great Teams*. Dallas, TX: The Pragmatic Programmers LLC.

Morgesen, F., et al. (2010) Leadership in Teams: A Functional Approach to Understanding Leadership Structures and Processes. *Journal of Management*, vol. 36, no. 1, pp. 5–39. https://doi.org/10.1177/0149206309347376.

Pelled, L. H., Eisenhardt, K. M., and Xin, K. R. (1999) Exploring the Black Box: An Analysis of Work Group Diversity, Conflict, and Performance. *Administrative Science Quarterly*, vol. 44, no. 1, pp. 1–28. JSTOR. www.jstor.org/stable/2667029. Accessed January 24, 2021.

Vozza, S. (2013) *How to Set Healthy Boundaries in the Workplace*. www.entrepreneur.com/article/230556. Accessed June 10, 2021.

Chapter 3

Falling into the trap of groupthink – how groups do their best thinking

The previous chapter explored how to create an excellent foundation for team coaching. Here we delve into the fascinating and challenging world of what drives human behaviour – a critical and essential topic for anyone working with people. Understanding what drives behaviour in groups will help inform your coaching and explain some of the behaviours you observe. Our principle of coaching the team in the room and the system they represent is especially relevant to this chapter. We are all subject to our world experiences and how we represent those experiences internally – either consciously or not. This quote from Koen Smets (2018) combines in one sentence the challenge we face when working with people.

> Human behaviour is complex, and sensitive to context and circumstances.

We like to think we are rational human beings capable of consistently making reasoned decisions and behaving in a thought-through and reasonable way. In the last 50 years, we know from research that this assumption is based on a shaky premise. Our behaviour is not always rational or driven by self-interest, as the classical economics model suggests. We are more likely to be driven by unconscious tendencies observed as biases and rules of thumb. That is, we're unaware of them. We now know that it takes conscious effort to behave rationally as we have a natural, pre-programmed behavioural tendency for bias.

A bias is a systematic error in our thinking that leads us to make poor quality decisions. But that's not the whole truth about biases. Thinking about the amount of data that bombard our brains on a second-by-second basis means we need some way of making decisions. The biases and rules of thumb that we operate with evolved to serve us. Technological, social and political advancements, it is argued, have made some of these natural biases problematic. Our evolutionary programming is lagging progress in our external world.

For teams working together, bias impacts performance in terms of not only the productivity output but also the interpersonal interactions within the team. We can describe some of the behaviours we observe when working with teams using the

DOI: 10.4324/9781003110583-4

terminology of bias and heuristics. Whilst this doesn't explain why the behaviour occurs, what it does help with is understanding some tactics we might use to reduce the effect of these tendencies.

It's essential to recognise that biases don't cause behaviour. They are descriptors for what we observe when working with teams and people in general. Another way of describing them is psychological phenomena. Therefore, we can never be certain why people behave the way they do, which is one of the challenges we have in navigating the complex workings of the mind. The second point to remember is that we can't predict biases and rules of thumb decision making. The thinking happens internally. We have no certainty about where those thoughts occur, the impact of the context on those thoughts and how our relationships with people on that specific day amplify or dampen cognitive processing. These two points, context and relationships, combined perhaps explain why working with people in social groupings is complex and how success one day with one team might not be replicable with the same team on another day!

Bias happens before we've engaged conscious thought and manifests in our actions, but there are some ways to slow down our thinking process to counteract some of these biases and rules of thumb decision making. For teams to work effectively together, they need to be vigilant to the adverse effects of human thinking and consciously use tools and techniques to help them do their best thinking. Additionally, they also need to understand how some of these biases might help them. Not all bias is bad – it's the context that determines the quality.

To help a team become self-organising, we as coaches need to help the team become aware of these limitations in our thinking. And that these limitations impact how we act. Moreover, our role is to help the team adopt an experimental approach to how they work together. Creating hypotheses and testing different interventions that acknowledge human behaviour's complexity also free the team to think deeper about working together.

This chapter explores some of the key biases we might observe when working with teams and how these behaviours affect a team's ability to work together optimally. Whilst groupthink is one of the more apparent biases we can observe, others also become problematic if a team is to work effectively together. Essentially working in a team requires us to know how we can do our best thinking. How will the team understand the likely pitfalls to look out for? One of the critical challenges for any team is the people within it! Many issues arise in teams because of unconscious thinking patterns, which then manifest in behaviours. We'll explore some of the more relevant ones to look out for, including:

- Groupthink
- Confirmation bias
- Status quo bias
- Authority bias
- Priming and anchoring

Whilst we can't eradicate bias, we can help the team create behavioural tactics to reduce their effect. The adage that you can't think your way into doing something different might seem trite here, but true. Only by systematically adapting our behaviour, will we effect changes in our thinking.

Having explored the biases and heuristics, we'll outline tools and techniques to help you coach teams, think and behave effectively together. These tools have the added benefit that they assist with helping the team discuss thorny issues and challenge thinking. We'll discuss in a later chapter one of the topics that usually come up when teams work together – conflict and how to have creative differences.

Some of the tools at the coach's disposal derive from 'thinking slow' – purposeful or deliberate practice, reflection and retrospectives. As you read through these biases, remember that they are descriptors of observed phenomena and not causes of the behaviour. Therefore, the tools and techniques that follow should be approached as experiments that you use with permission and co-create with the team.

3.1 Groupthink – don't rock the boat

You've probably heard of the term groupthink before and probably thought you're not affected by it. The reality is that we're all affected by groupthink because it's something that happens at an unconscious level.

It's natural for most of us to want to fit in and feel part of the group. The tendency that individuals in a group will sacrifice challenging decisions and voicing dissent for harmony and consensus is the positive intent behind the behaviour. Sometimes, this is what the team needs. At other times, this behaviour isn't helpful. By conforming to the majority view, the group demonstrates the belief they are reducing conflict and disagreement yet might be sacrificing better decision making and a more beneficial outcome.

Not speaking up and offering an alternative position or voicing concerns can ultimately lead teams to go down rabbit holes when working on challenging tasks. In some cases, it can also lead to wasted time and energy on the wrong solutions. It is perhaps one of the most pernicious tendencies for stifling creativity and innovation precisely because alternatives are hard to come by if the majority becomes fixed on a solution.

It's also a convenient way of avoiding conflict and ostensibly keeping harmony in the group. Often there are underlying tensions that creep in through the back door and manifest as side-conversations, sabotage and backbiting. It's also a breeding ground for power struggles within the team.

Paradoxically, groupthink is one of the critical factors in group conflict. When a group seemingly agrees too much, that is usually a leading indicator that something is likely to happen in the future to derail the team. It is essential to have effective tactics for keeping conflict creative and productive.

One team I worked with on the surface seemed to work well together, with minimal disagreement. At first, it was unsettling to work with this team because they had their language. Over time, as they trusted me more, individually, they would share their concerns and grievances but only one on one. It was clear that many of the decisions were made by one person, with minimal dissent.

In hindsight, authority bias was likely at play here and the team's lack of psychological safety. Despite my best efforts to help the team have the conversations in the group versus with me, the grievances manifest in deviant behaviours within the team. Eventually, the veneer of harmony peeled away as the team crumbled into dysfunction.

3.2   Confirmation bias – seeing what you want to see

Next to groupthink, confirmation bias – the tendency to seek proof for our beliefs – is another potential source of group conflict. Often doubling down when those beliefs are challenged, team members voraciously search for evidence to support their view.

This bias manifests in pet theories and silver bullets, to use the vernacular, quoting a single point of reference not based on scientific research but one which supports the holder's point of view. The behaviour stems from a firmly held belief that they seek to prove. The person quoting the source defends their position vigorously in the face of contrary data. Sometimes, this challenge enflames the individual to find more confirmatory evidence for their point of view. This behaviour is particularly challenging if the person has authority through position or status within the team.

Countering our natural inclination to rush to judgement is vital to improving decision making. As coaches, we can challenge the team's thinking and check to see what evidence exists, both quantity and quality, to support a course of action. One of the tools discussed later helps counter this behaviour.

Six Sigma has a certain brand value which attracts kudos to organisations that introduce it. One team member wanted to introduce Six Sigma because they'd heard good things about it and felt that we could achieve more by adopting this methodology. It was my job to investigate.

3.3 Status quo bias – stick with what you know

The 'do nothing' option can feel safer to teams, particularly if they're challenged to develop new or different solutions. Changing work practices are necessary for teams to adapt to working more autonomously. Self-organising teams must be open to challenging previous ways of working. Status quo bias is the tendency to stick with the safe option, which is usually the option you already know. This tendency can often take the form of 'why fix it if it isn't broke' or similar words.

The team will potentially act in this way in the early stages of forming together. It's much easier to fall back onto well-known practices than it is to learn new ones. Not only does it require greater mental energy, but there is also another effect – loss aversion – impacting our willingness to do something different.

We don't like to lose something that we know, and if we lose it, it takes on greater significance and value. Loss aversion is where the pain of the loss is perceived as more significant than the gains of something new. The combined tendencies towards the status quo and loss aversion contribute to demonstrable team inertia and lack of willingness to try new things.

For a coach, this can be challenging since our role is to help the team grow. As we know, growth occurs at the edge of our comfort zone. It's therefore in the team's interest to identify these tendencies early to reduce the impact on performance. Surfacing these concerns and giving voice to them help reduce their impact and assist with identifying tactics for countering them.

3.4 Authority bias – perceived status counts

Self-organising teams are not necessarily free from hierarchy – perceived or real. Often there is one role that carries weight in an organisation. Buffer found that people naturally gravitate towards the experienced person in the room, the one with the best skills or who can provide guidance and direction for the team.

The tendency to give greater weight to the opinions of others we perceive who have authority and our willingness to be influenced by them makes sense when the team is forming. After all, we ask who has knowledge or skills in this area for a reason – we want to be certain that we're moving in the right direction.

The downside is when we automatically attribute credit and are influenced by people within the team because of their perceived position. It may be that the most experienced developer in the room is the person to lead a discussion about the technical aspects of a solution. Taking the lead from this person makes sense because they have skills in this area. However, this becomes problematic when the default is to listen to one person's viewpoint every time.

Our automatic, unconscious response to authority figures within the team might not make sense if we seek alternative or novel solutions to problems. The coach's role is to help the team seek alternative viewpoints and help them be vigilant to patterns of behaviour that steer the team to one person.

3.5   Priming and anchoring – get what you expect

These two seem to go together – another way of thinking about priming is pre-framing. There is a tendency for the brain to make associative links, unconsciously, based on primed words or experiences.

Priming is a global term covering the associative workings of the mind. Think of it as a suggestion starter. In Kahneman's book (2011), he describes many different types of priming, the upshot of all these types of priming is that we respond to cues and our mind makes associations based on those cues. These associations, in turn, affect our behaviour. For example, in one experiment, the Florida Experiment, students were asked to create phrases from words associated with older people. The researchers observed the people walking immediately after the priming. The researchers observed these students walked more slowly after the word association experiment.

This phenomenon is interesting for teams to explore since the way they speak and the language they use to work together might create a tendency to prime behaviour. In coaching, we are aware of the impact of language on our behaviour. The internal dialogue we speak to ourselves shapes our self-image and how we perceive others.

It is easy for teams to follow instructions without realising the potential for being led in one direction. Another experiment, not specifically around priming, demonstrates how our unconscious mind operates – even when we endeavour to activate conscious cognitive processing.

Spot the gorilla

Research published in 2013 by three social psychologists (Drew et al. 2013) highlighted some interesting facts about how we see data. They asked 24 radiologists to carry out a well-known lung-node detection test on a series of X-rays. Unbeknown to the radiologist in the last X-ray, the scientists had added an image of a gorilla 48 times larger than the lung nodule they were looking for. And what they found was that 83% of the radiologists missed the gorilla on that last test case. Using eye-tracking technology, they knew that 20 radiologists had looked straight at it!

They concluded that even when working in an area of familiar expertise, we are still subject to something called inattentional blindness, i.e. not spotting something in full view because our attention is elsewhere.

Anchoring

The related tendency to priming is anchoring –

> 'It occurs when people consider a particular value for an unknown quantity before estimating that quantity'.

For teams, this can be a challenge since planning work and estimating timeframes require careful consideration. Budgets and timeframes are two key metrics teams are often measured on – if there is already a view on the table, these will influence the team's behaviour, even if there is ostensibly freedom for the team to set their own.

In this way, the initial number acts as a priming tendency which the team will unconsciously anchor. In organisations, this happens frequently and can be the source of frustration within teams. The unconscious influence that the first number has on the team means they must work hard at setting them aside.

3.6 Tools and techniques

Having explored some of the biases that make us perfectly flawed human beings, let's discover some of the ways we can help the team develop constructive behaviours. These tools help counter some of our natural tendencies. As you will have realised, though, there is no magic wand or silver bullet. Coaching teams is about assisting them to discover their ways of becoming a fully functioning team based on growth and experimentation. Context, as they say, is king. The following tips and tools are starting points to help trigger the learning process for the team. They are not designed as t*he solution* but as possible solutions that might help get you started.

3.7 Complex or obvious problems

The first tool is based on the Cynefin framework of Dave Snowden and created to help the team work out which decisions require deep-level thinking to reduce bias. Some decisions will make sense immediately and are based on clear cause and effect, whereas other decisions will be more complex where there is no obvious cause and effect. The team needs a simple way of identifying where to spend effort.

In the following diagram,

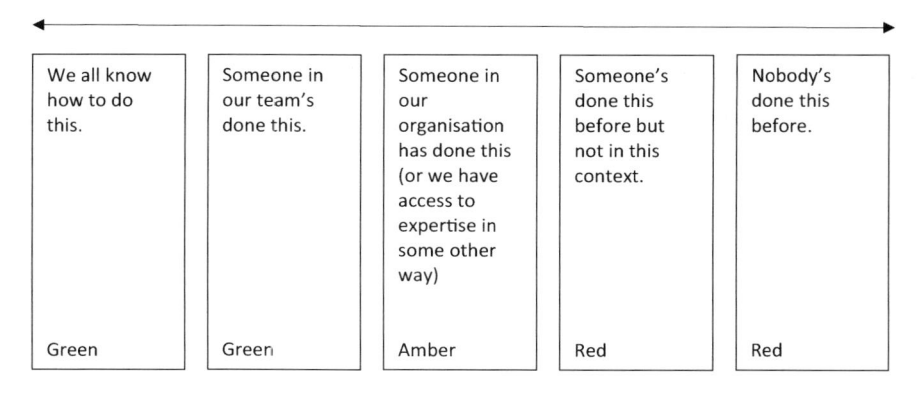

Figure 3.1 Contextual Decision Making

I've suggested using a sliding scale to identify where the decision or problem lies. The questions provided by Liz Keogh from her blog post *Cynefin For Everyone* are an excellent resource. Using a slider helps the group create an initial view on the decision, challenge or problem. The coach's role is to present the tool and help the team discuss the problem so that assumptions come to the surface. The team might already know the answer to the questions, in which case the slider is redundant. The questions in the red boxes are different from the others in they denote complexity and potentially chaotic. For example, the initial experiences in the COVID-19 pandemic fell into the chaotic domain of decision making – the world had to make decisions in a time of crisis, with no known current solution. Significantly few people are still alive from the pandemic of the early twentieth century, so decision making was more in the act, sense, respond mode.

Draw the slider on a piece of flipchart paper and put it on a wall. Ask people to mark where they think the topic in question sits on the slider and facilitate the conversation around the assumptions and knowledge that is within the team. If there is a view that the decision or problem is an obvious one, challenge the team to identify examples. Where specifically? How often? Qualify the type of problem upfront, so the team allocates appropriate time and effort to decisions or problems that need them.

3.8 Which bias might we encounter?

Spending time on the things that will deliver benefit is part of the learning process for any team. Identifying the nature of the problem or decision upfront means that the team can create tactics to reduce bias in thinking. Here are some tips for countering bias in thinking – as the team matures and learns about how the biases manifest in their scenario, these can be tweaked and updated.

3.9 Check the source

Countering biases like confirmation bias or optimism bias requires scrutiny of sources of information and expertise. Not all sources are created equal. For example, newspaper articles that headline the latest cure for 'XYZ ailment' usually derive from one source. Often, the writer will cherry-pick headline-worthy quotes to ignite reader interest.

As a coach, you can help the team become more selective about data sources and help them develop an evidence-based approach. In their groundbreaking, *Harvard Business Review* article, Jeffrey Pfeffer and Sutton (2006) outline an evidence-based approach in Management. Countering bias requires 'slower' thinking. Many organisations are action-biased – seeking action over-analysis,

Table 3.1 Tip for Countering Biases

Optimism or Over-Confidence Bias	Group Think	Confirmation Bias	Anchoring	Priming	Loss Aversion	Status Quo
Look for examples where things have not gone well	Actively seek dissenting views in the group	Actively seek alternative dissenting views in the group	Physically place the number or viewpoint to one side – write it or draw and put that piece of paper in a different part of the room before discussing	Notice what is physically in your environment – posters on walls, on desks, on your screens. Might they be priming your thinking in some way?	If the decision has potential large downsides, think about how to break it down into smaller micro-decisions with smaller losses	Use Cartesian logic to identify best- and worst-case scenarios
Clarify what 'best' case scenario means	Appoint a Devil's advocate	Suspend judgement until all data have been reviewed	Decide if you want to use an anchor – this could be viewed a form of constraint, e.g. amount of time and amount of budget	Find somewhere neutral to have important conversations requiring deep thought – off site, virtual	Create pilot or test projects to limit the risk of loss	Identify one small step to move forward
Conduct pre-mortems (see later)	Use anonymous voting to check for agreement	Find ways to take out data that might influence decisions, e.g. only look at data that is relevant to the problem or decision in hand	Carry or a pre-mortem.	What guidelines have you been given? What is the source of these? Might they be influencing your thinking? Can you put these to one side?	Carry out a pre-mortem to identify what might be at stake	Identify what the obstacles are stopping the team from doing something different and what the enablers might be to help take that first step (force field analysis)
Outline worst-case scenarios	Ask people to write down their viewpoint first before discussing, go around the room individually to hear each other's point of view before opening general discussion	Look for contradictory data			Put the loss in context – if the decision the team is making is part of a bigger project what proportion of the project might this loss impact?	
Research evidence to test outcomes both good and bad		Use the Devil's Advocate technique (see later)				
Identify examples in the organisation, if possible, where things have gone well and not so well						

and this relies on intuitive and quick thinking. To help the team reduce the tendency towards bias requires careful coaching to develop a more selective approach to the data. Here's a simple checklist.

Expert input:

> How often has the expert done this particular thing?
> What was the context in which they did this particular thing?
> What feedback did the expert receive? (Were there any criteria they were working to?)
> What were the results they achieved?
> Were these results achieved every time they did this particular thing?

Research:

> What is the source of the research?
> Is the research peer-reviewed?
> Is the research based on a sound research method?
> Has the research been validated through replicable experiments?

Check the context

Context is king! We will visit this theme many times because it's important to remember that coaching self-organising teams is influenced by context. As coaches, we can sometimes live in our own biases too much and rely too heavily on one approach or toolset simply because it has worked in the past. We must guard against this kind of thinking and check our behaviour, basing our actions instead on what we see and experience with each team.

One of the tools my business partner and I use a lot is the Lean Change toolkit developed by Jason Little. It's a simple set of sliders measuring different aspects of an organisation. The ones listed in the figure are suggestions. There might be different ones you wish to use with the team.

Draw the following diagram on a flipchart. Ask the team to assess, individually, where they think the organisation sits on each of the continua. To avoid groupthink, you could ask them to draw it on a piece of paper and collect each answer. You, as the coach, then plot everyone's response on the flipchart paper. Your role is to prompt a conversation about the different views and tease out the reasons behind the scoring.

The output of the discussions then informs how the group will make decisions, be influenced by the organisational context and come up with ideas to counter any inherent biases that might be apparent.

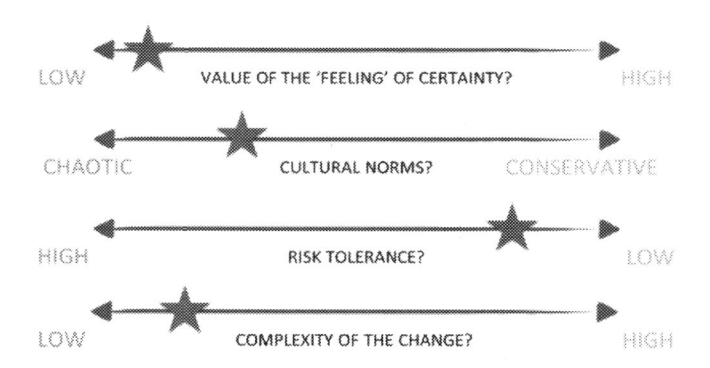

Figure 3.2 Defining the Context

3.10 The devil's advocate

The devil's advocate is a concept steeped in historical context based on the Catholic Church's legal advocate from the sixteenth century who would argue against the canonisation of a candidate. The relevance of this archaic tool is that it helps teams argue the other side for any possible decision. It is a debating device designed to position the opposing view.

Before using the tool, the team has to have set up enough safety and have robust ground rules. The very nature of the tool means that it invites conflict. One possible ground rule is that it is the idea, decision, approach, etc., that the team interrogates, not the person. This safety net helps to de-focus it from a personal attack.

The team selects one person to act as the advocate whose role is to critique and question assumptions about a decision or an approach. They can ask any question, dig deep by probing for more information, supporting evidence, assumptions and so on.

The team will know when emotional 'hot buttons' are triggered through the advocacy process, indicating areas for further investigation. Your role as a coach is to help keep the conversation positive yet robust.

3.11 Cartesian logic

Our mind looks for ways to conserve energy, and this simple tool has had many coaching clients flummoxed and questioning what they thought they understood. It's based on the work of Rene Descartes and is a set of four questions that you ask. It's represented here as a four-box model because this is easy to draw on the flipchart paper.

Using the flipchart paper to draw out the grid helps to work through the questions and can also be used with sticky notes to capture conversations. One

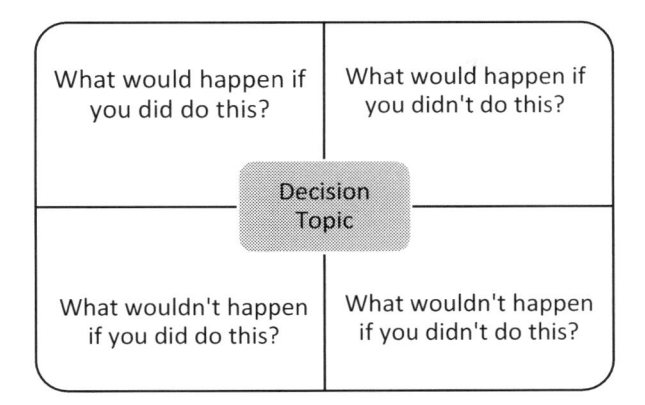

Figure 3.3 Cartesian Logic

coaching client used this approach and prioritised the different sticky notes afterwards, which then helped with action planning.

The key is that the questions direct the conversation and create insights and further investigation. They help with 'thinking slow' and stop us in our tracks – a great way of countering bias and running with mental shortcuts.

3.12 Pre-mortems or prospective hindsight

Professor Gary Klein developed the term and approach for pre-mortems, and in a similar vein, J. Edward Russo and Paul Schoemaker developed Prospective Hindsight. Both deal with the same thing – stepping into the future and identifying everything that could have possibly gone wrong and countering with what has gone well.

I have used this approach for both positive and negative projections of the future. I blend the activity with movement, asking teams to move to space in the room representing the future. This spatial element has had the added benefit of creating both literal and mental distance between the present and the future.

Once in the future, each team member identifies everything that has gone wrong. Using sticky notes, one per thought makes it easier to put things on a wall to discuss once the initial thinking and writing process is complete. Between 5 and 10 minutes usually gives enough time.

When everyone has written up their thoughts, they post them on the wall – the team can now theme these. For example, communication might come up as a generic topic (it would be surprising if it didn't!). This theming activity helps the team do a quick sort of the topics to help the discussion flow and plan what to do with the outputs.

After the discussion, there will be key points that emerge and natural actions that follow. There might also be 'don't knows' – these become follow-up points for the team to find out more.

Taking the team to a point in the future frees up thinking about the problems and challenges in the current day, helps them think broader about what might happen and creates some insight into what is known and unknown through discussion.

3.13 Summary

Biases serve us well most of the time. They help us sort the wheat from the chaff in making day-to-day decisions. They become problematic when we add in complexity. Working in self-organising teams within a larger organisation creates complexity. Making decisions in areas where the variables might be unknown, complicated or more challenging to calculate increases the chances that we will behave in less than rational ways.

Reducing the negative downsides of bias is how we as coaches can help self-organising teams by increasing knowledge of how biases operate and develop behavioural tactics. As I outlined at the beginning of this chapter, only by adapting our behaviour systematically, we will effect changes in our thinking.

- Biases don't cause behaviour. They are descriptors for what we observe. We can never be sure why people behave the way they do.
- It takes conscious effort to behave rationally. We help the team become aware of the limitations on our thinking, but we cannot know which biases are likely to show up.
- Five biases that show up in coaching teams:
  - Groupthink
  - Confirmation bias
  - Status quo bias
  - Authority bias
  - Priming and anchoring.
- Establish in which domain the team's challenge lies. Establishing this will help the team determine what responses they take and suggested pathways for decision making.
- Develop a set of tactics to help counter natural bias in thinking. The tool on Tips for Countering bias acts as a starting point for the team to develop a set of their own.
- Help the team create an evidence-based approach to working. Educate the team on the core principles and invite them to discuss how they might adopt them as a team.
- Acknowledge bias in yourself and use reflection activities to understand how you can reduce their impact when coaching teams.

- Experiment often using a systematic approach. For example, develop a hypothesis, use approaches and tools to test the hypothesis and capture what you learn. A great way of doing this, as we know, is through regular retrospectives. That is, the team does a periodic review of how things are going, what they're learning, what insights they have had, what successes they've had and so on.
- Remember the importance of context – what works in one place and time might not work in the same place at a different time.

Bibliography

Drew T.-Vo, M. L. H., and Wolfe, J. M. (2013) The Invisible Gorilla Strikes Again: Sustained Inattentional Blindness in Expert Observers. *Psychological Science*, vol. 24, no. 9, pp. 1848–1853. https://journals.sagepub.com/doi/10.1177/0956797613479386?url_ver=Z39.88-2003&rfr_id=ori:rid:crossref.org&rfr_dat=cr_pub%3dpubmed. Accessed June 10, 2021.

Kahneman, D. (2011) *Thinking, Fast and Slow*. New York, NY: Farrar, Straus and Giroux.

Keogh, L. *Cynefin for Everyone*. https://lizkeogh.com/cynefin-for-everyone/. Accessed January 1, 2021.

Little, J. *Lean Change Toolkit*. Lean Change Association. leanchange.org.

Pfeffer, J., and Sutton, R. I. (2006) Evidence Based Management. *Harvard Business Review*. https://hbr.org/2006/01/evidence-based-management. Accessed June 11, 2021.

Shiller, R. (2016) *Irrational Exuberance*. Princeton, NJ: Princeton University Press.

Simon, H. A. (1990) Bounded Rationality. In: Eatwell, J., Milgate, M., and Newman, P. (eds.), *Utility and Probability. The New Palgrave*. London: Palgrave Macmillan. https://doi.org/10.1007/978-1-349-20568-4_5.

Smets, K. (2018) *There Is More to Behavioral Economics Than Biases and Fallacies*. https://behavioralscientist.org/there-is-more-to-behavioral-science-than-biases-and-fallacies/. Accessed November 21, 2019.

Snowden, D. J., and Boone, M. E. (2007) A Leadership Framework for Decision Making. *Harvard Business Review*. https://hbr.org/2007/11/a-leaders-framework-for-decision-making. Accessed January 25, 2021.

Thaler, R., and Sunstein, C. (2009) *Nudge: Improving Decisions about Health, Wealth and Happiness*. London: Penguin Group.

Widrich, L. (2015) *What We Got Wrong About Self-Management: Embracing Natural Hierarchy at Work*. https://open.buffer.com/self-management-hierarchy/. Accessed January 25, 2019.

Chapter 4

How to handle disagreements and conflict

You have likely been involved in a conflict at work at some stage in your career – either minor disagreements on how a piece of work is performed or, at the other end of the spectrum, an out and out shouting match.

Conflict is part of the human condition. We see it in adversarial political debates and differences of opinions to individual personal relationships. If you think of the word conflict, what does it conjure up for you? Likely you will have a mental model of what it means and a natural inclination to avoid or accept it. Mental models create our reality. The upside to this means conflict doesn't have to be negative. If we explore our mental models about conflict, we can find different approaches for reaching our goals – both individually and within the team.

Helping teams cope with and work through conflicts is one of the necessary parts of coaching self-organising teams. For us, as coaches, this can be both challenging and rewarding. Sitting with the team in the discomfort of conflict requires not only skill but our willingness to let go of control and help the team navigate their way through to resolution – if possible and desirable. With care and practice, teams can learn how to navigate these choppy waters and sail to the sunny shores of creativity and innovation. Without conflict, we would never leave our comfort zone and explore alternatives. Adopting a mental model of conflict as natural ebb and flow provides an opportunity for exploration and growth.

Contracting and creating a psychologically safe space are the foundation stones for building conflict as a force for creativity. Teams that lack an explicit agreement on how they will handle challenges and create a safe environment to question and speak up will struggle with conflict. The coaching contract with the team is also pivotal in how the coach will help and support the team as it works through likely disputes.

In this chapter, we explore:

- What conflict is
- How we can frame the definition
- Sources of conflict and the warning signs of crisis
- How to harness conflict and turn it into a force for creation and innovation
- How to help teams navigate away from crisis and use conflict as an opportunity for growth

DOI: 10.4324/9781003110583-5

4.1   What is conflict?

As a lapsed Classics scholar, my starting point for understanding any word is understanding etymology. Conflict comes from two words: Con fligere – the Latin for 'to strike together'. For me, this creates the metaphor of two pieces of flint striking together to cause a spark and following this metaphor through, when navigating conflict positively, that spark produces energy and creativity. The metaphor creates images of a warm fire on a cold day, a source for cooking and a means of melting metals to make resources for building. Using our imagination, we can see the positive intent of conflict.

On the other side when a spark is left unchecked, it quickly ignites flammable materials in its path and readily burns out of control. Now we have a crisis.

Conflict, put simply, is a difference of two or more opinions, perspectives, mental models and so on that have created a sticking point. A disagreement that becomes a sticking point, or spark, needs to find a path to resolution or escalation.

We often shy away from discussing conflict for many reasons. Some are cultural, others are learned behaviours, for example, 'we don't wash our dirty linen in public'. Asking teams to develop a metaphor for conflict and following the metaphor through, as demonstrated earlier, is one way to start the conversation. Helping the team explore their insights about what conflict means for them individually and how it might play out in the team helps name the 'elephant in the room' safely. Questions naturally arise:

* What are the implications of how we work through conflict in this team?
* How might conflict show up?

The team can potentially create their potential sources of conflict, which is where we go next.

Sources of conflict

Likely, one source of conflict will readily emerge from conversations about the topic – relationships. In workshops, this usually comes up as the first point when discussing conflict, resistance and disagreements. Yet, it's not the only source of conflict. In the following diagram, I outline four sources of conflict and how they might occur. These sources of conflict stem from different research and observations of working with teams. It provides a starting point for discussion. It's not intended to be exhaustive, nor is it intended as the single source of truth. Use it as a model to design activities and tools to help teams gain insight into the possible reasons for the conflict to help them find a pathway.

One field of study that sheds light on potential sources of conflict is transactional analysis created by Eric Berne and is a theory of personality, a model of communication and a study of repetitive behaviour patterns. Identity plays a

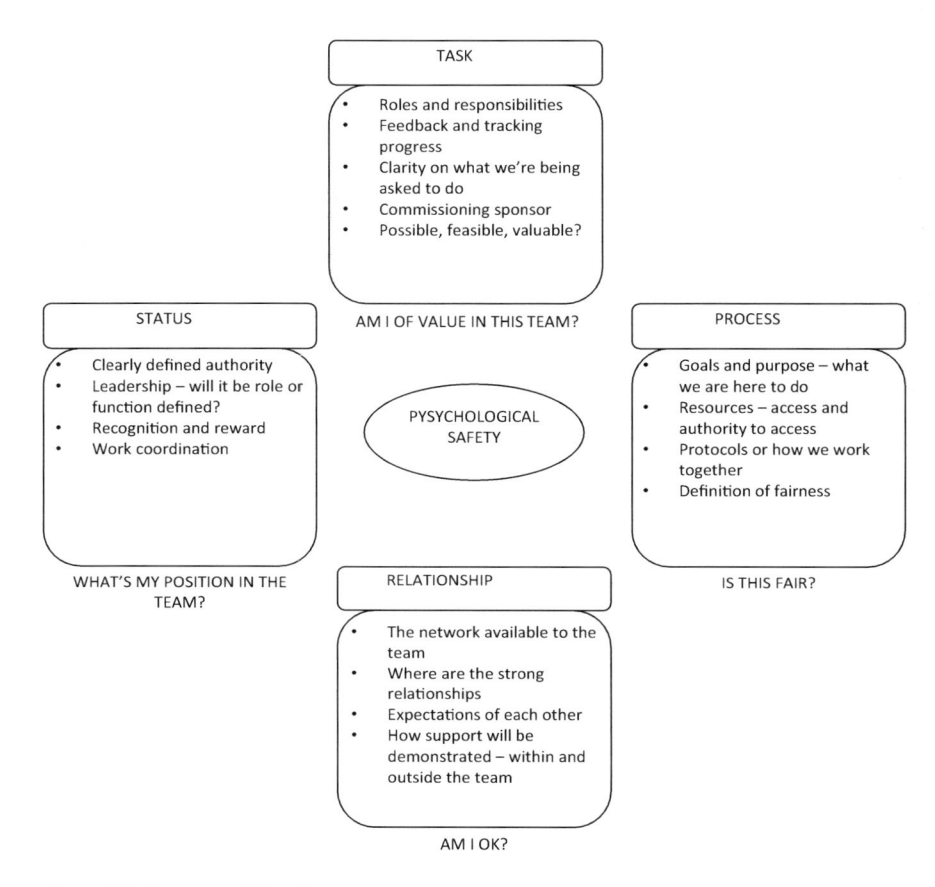

Figure 4.1 Sources of Conflict

driving role in task-based sources of conflict because the focus is on how much I am valued. Is what I'm doing making a difference?

If we don't know what we're meant to be doing and nobody is taking any notice of what we're doing, or we do something, and it gets put to one side without being used, it impacts our sense of self-worth – that we're not bringing anything to the table that's of value.

The second one is around process conflict. The process is about how the team works together.

- What protocols does the team have?
- What processes does the team have?
- How often does the team meet?

Ultimately, this is about making sure that whatever you're doing together as a team, everybody feels it's fair. Fairness goes to the heart of who we are as individuals.

The fair process effect phenomenon (Van Den Bos et al. 1998) found that procedural fairness matters more when we can't judge the outcomes we receive relative to others. Weighing up factors such as perceived contribution rate compared with others means that we are more likely to judge situations based on how satisfied we are with the outcome. Therefore, relative fairness based on outcomes can be a potential source of conflict if one person in the team feels 'hard done' compared to their teammates.

In the field of organisation development in the work of Edgar Schein and others, procedural fairness drives behaviours not only in teams but more widely in organisations. Making sure that people feel there's a fair process for the team to work together is essential. Based on the research of Van Den Bos and colleagues, satisfaction with outcomes in comparison with others is a significant driver. This latter point is more about outcome favourability and satisfaction. As a team coach, this phenomenon can be challenging because we want the team to create a shared view of outcomes. The collective outcomes become more significant than the individual. In this respect, procedural fairness will play out in how teams compare their outcomes versus other teams' outcomes. It is perhaps one reason we observe silo thinking in organisations where strongly aligned teams become resentful of contributing to the organisation's greater good, particularly where they are offsetting teams who are not performing as well.

In my experience of working in organisational change, people can tolerate many changes and decisions. Still, once there is a perceived injustice or unfairness, it sparks a rallying cry even if the perceived unfairness is not perpetrated against the individual personally. Expectations and procedural fairness lie beneath the surface in the realm of the psychological contract. The nature of the exchange relationship is that I give something to you in anticipation of receiving something in return. You can use this lens to help the team understand what exchange relationships they create within the team and other stakeholders. Relationships are the third potential source of conflict.

Implied in the word relationships is how we relate to others, which indicates how we compare ourselves to others. Returning to Transactional Analysis, the OK Corral model (Ernst 1971) looks at the various states of being OK or not OK.

- Am I OK with this team?
- Are you OK with this team?
- Are we OK together?

For teams to operate at optimal levels around conflict, the aiming point is one of – I am OK and you are OK. Being comfortable with ourselves and others means, we can talk together on an adult-to-adult basis rather than a parent to a child where we might be infantilising the other person or chastising them and at the other extreme critical parent to a rebellious child where we are in telling mode and the other person is actively resisting.

If someone feels they're not OK, but everyone else is OK, that can lead to the individual feeling victimised, often expressed as 'you just don't get where I'm coming from' or 'why is everyone against me?' On the other hand, if someone feels OK and believes everyone else is at fault, that can lead to blame and aggression. This state can sometimes sound like 'what don't you get, it's simple' or 'I'm the expert on this, just do it!' The trickiest state to deal with is when someone feels they're not OK and perceives everyone else is not OK too – this leads to enlisting others into their downward spiral of despair.

Often conflict links with more than one area. Once it surfaces, it is easy to label it as a 'relationship' issue. Helping the team identify the real source of the problem makes resolution or amelioration possible. In Chapter 5, we will explore a tool for helping the team do this. Your role as the team coach makes it likely you will at some stage have a conversation with a team member that presents as a 'relationship' issue with another team member. One of the first questions I ask in these situations is 'What have you done so far to resolve the situation?' Our role as coaches is to help the team learn how to resolve their issues by enabling team members to take actions themselves. If the person seeking your help hasn't taken any action so far, a quick coaching conversation to help them work out what they could and will do next provides a learning opportunity. Depending on the situation presented, it might require further intervention between the two team members. The team might also need to address a systemic issue and even a broader organisational issue. The key is not to step in and 'rescue' the team member by taking action.

Many years ago, I was part of a team where one team member had an undeclared issue with another team member over how much 'airtime' they had in meetings. It transpired during one coaching session that one member had spoken with the coach, who was now raising it with the team. Unfortunately, the other person had no idea that it was an issue and was unaware the coach would present it at the session. On the receiving end of the perceived criticism, the team member seemed utterly blindsided by the presenting problem and no doubt felt extremely uncomfortable and vulnerable. It didn't go well and resulted in that person leaving the room. It was a great learning point for the remaining members of the team, although the coach and team could have had a more productive result had it been approached differently.

It is clear that the positive intent of the coach was to help the situation, and they made a judgement call to 'bring it to the team'. However, it felt extremely uncomfortable being a spectator in this scenario. The coach did have other options. They could have facilitated a conversation between the two people separately. Any system-related issues that came out of this conversation could then be brought back into the team for broader discussion. The coach could have suggested the person speak with the other person first if they felt confident enough to do that. In this situation, the sources of potential conflict were the process, and this then mutated into the relationship. After that session, it became almost impossible for them to rebuild their relationship.

Team membership, who is in the team, can be as much a source of conflict as relationships. If team membership is stable over time, this presents opportunities to develop healthy relationships. It also creates the space for the resolution of issues. If team membership is fluid, the introduction of new team members can unwittingly create an additional potential source of conflict – particularly if the onboarding of the new team member is not well planned. Every time someone joins the team, the coach must re-contract with the team and help the team learn how to do this. As we learnt in a previous chapter, 'extreme teaming' is becoming more prevalent as organisations seek to mobilise project resources at short notice and expect effective results. In one organisation that adopts a holacracy model, it is possible to be a member of more than one team and for teams to move around depending on projects available. Membership of multiple teams creates another layer of complexity for the team coach because team members will likely not have 100% of their time allocated to a single team.

Team fluidity in holacratic organisations

Individuals can be members of multiple teams. Assuming a 100% allocation, this can be spread across different teams, e.g. 20% of time allocated to Team 1, 30% allocated to Team 2, etc. Team leads negotiate the time required to agree on how much of the individual's allocation is available to the team.

It's possible to be a member of at least two teams or more at any one time.

Working in a team in a complex environment tests the coach's skills and exaggerates the natural tendencies of team members. The previous stories raise an important point about conflict – our natural tendency concerning conflict. Do you naturally seek to avoid it or confront it? Gallo (2017) explores this and how it might impact the end goal of what we aim to achieve. In the previous scenario, the end goal of raising the topic with the team wasn't clear. If it was to preserve relationships, then it achieved the exact opposite. Later in the chapter, we will explore the notion of conflict avoidance – not as a strategy but as a default natural tendency and how this can diminish the potential within the team.

The following figure offers a sliding scale to help you identify whether your natural tendency might be one of avoidance or provocateur. Some coaches purposely provoke conflict, particularly where a team has been stuck in a rut and not moving forward. At this end of the spectrum, this natural tendency can be helpful for teams where there is no conflict, and neither is there any energy. The team has reached a state of inertia and lethargy. However, as a coach, we should be wary of

Avoiding   Confronting   Provoking

Figure 4.2 Conflict Tendencies

sitting in our comfort zone. The provocateur approach might be comfortable for you. The key is to know when and how often to use it with the team.

You can also use this as a starting point for discussion with the team. Ask the team to self-assess individual and team natural style and share with the team. Turn it into a learning point by starting a conversation on when and how these natural tendencies might show up and how the team can use them as a resource.

Having explored the sources of conflict, let's turn to how conflict evolves and the implications for the team. A helpful model for understanding this is Glasl's (2004) model of conflict escalation, which he describes as a ladder of descent into ever-deepening conflict.

(Reprinted and updated with English translation with permission from 'Conflict management. A handbook for managers and consultants, 8th updated and supplemented edition', Paul Haupt Bern Stuttgart Vienna, Free Spiritual Life Stuttgart, 2004)

The nine stages have three categories:

- Win: win
- Win: lose
- Lose: lose

At the top of the ladder, it is still possible to resolve the conflict and attain a win: win outcome. If a team is at stages 1 through 3, it is still possible to resolve without outside help. As the conflict escalates, it is less likely to reach a resolution between the two parties. The external intervention of a third party is necessary.

This model is helpful to understand in coaching teams and emphasises the point of addressing differences of opinions and disputes early in the escalation process. It is also important to note that conflict can be across different teams. We are always coaching the system in which the team works, and this complexity makes addressing the conflict challenging. The team may well have to work together on both their conflict resolution tactics and develop tactics to resolve conflict with other teams and stakeholders.

Another model I came across many years ago was one based on expectations. In the early stages of a relationship, we have expectations of the other party or parties that are usually undeclared. Over time, these undeclared expectations, or assumptions, are tested by the actions of the other. As each expectation is unmet, we start to build grievances. As the resentments build, we become less tolerant until the pressure becomes so strong that we experience an emotional meltdown.

In the chapter on creating agreements with the team, we talked about how we are constantly testing the boundaries of these agreements and often need to reset

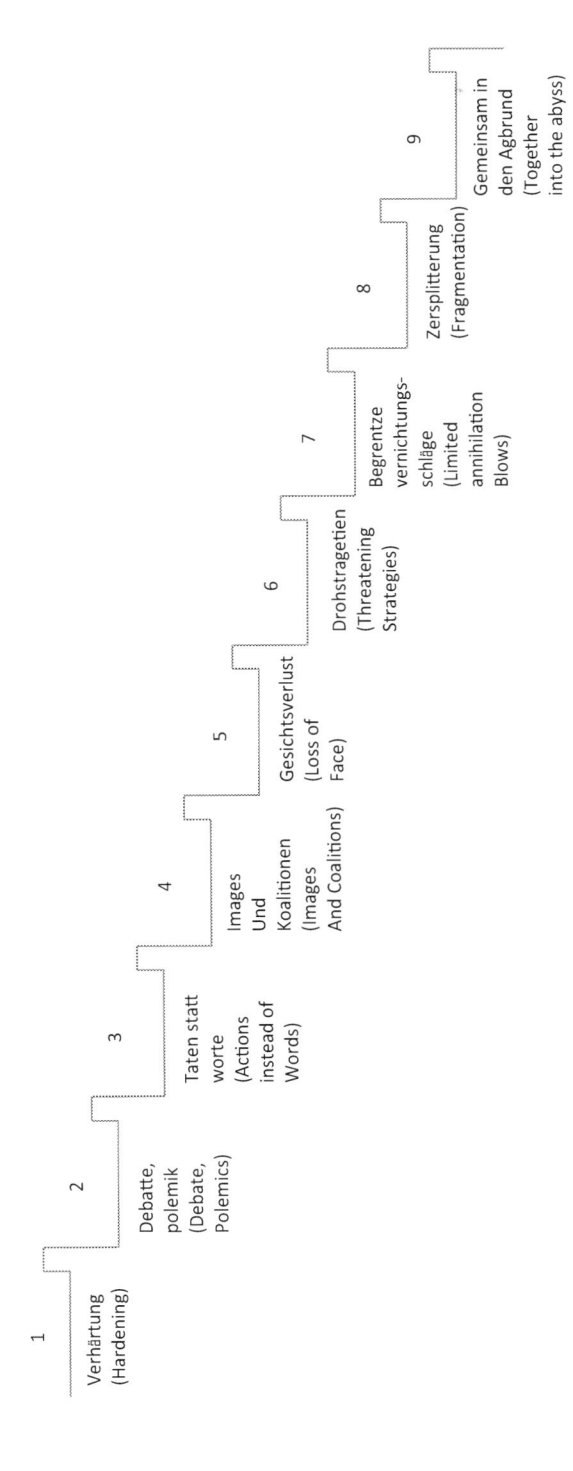

Figure 4.3 Model of Conflict Escalation (Glasl, 2004)

Table 4.1 Surfacing Expectations

What I expect from this team	What the team can expect from me	What I expect from my stakeholders	What my stakeholders can expect from me
Respect for the knowledge I bring	I will do my best and always offer evidence-based information	To respect the team's expertise	To act on the best available information

them as we learn more about how the team works together and consider new information that comes into the team. We know that we cannot halt the path of change, and teams are likely to develop skills to adapt to changing requirements. A simple way of making expectations explicit is to list them. See Table 4.1 for a suggested way to do this.

Models are imperfect representations of reality, but they serve as a guide to indicate action and approach. The more we can help the team surface expectations and assumptions, the less likely the minor differences in opinions will lead to significant fallings-out. Surfacing assumptions leads us to the next topic around conflict, that of avoidance.

4.2   Conflict avoidance and how it diminishes potential

It sometimes seems the best course of action to avoid open conflict. Avoidance is indeed a strategy, however, only if it is by choice. If avoidance is a natural inclination because the team is too afraid or lacks the confidence to challenge, it can become a potential for problems downstream. Many years ago, I worked with a team, or more accurately a group, that was so concerned with keeping everything professional, but the underlying issues affected performance. First, the 'team' was a collection of 15 people under a functional manager. This confusion of team or group was the first port of call – who was actually in the team? And what purpose did the 'team' follow? The manifesting problems were relationships. Relationships were why my colleague and I started working with the team and the client's description of the problem. In those days, I still used the Myers Briggs Type Indicator to help teams understand different preferences. More on this will be discussed later.

We set out by asking the team to complete the questionnaires and then did one-on-one follow-up sessions to feedback on their results and ask them their thoughts on the team and how we might help. We worked with the team month-by-month basis for around three months, following the relationship path as the source of the conflict. In one session, we ventured into the unspoken assumptions and 'elephants in the room'. During this session, it became clear that the unspoken grievances were hampering the team and whilst the session was 'robust', it at least laid out some of the reasons why the team was less than effective.

With hindsight, our approach would have been different. One of the sources of conflict was likely the size of the team. Another source was the purpose the team was seeking to achieve. As a collection of high-performing individuals, they were unlikely to succeed in working as a team without this overriding reason – the task they were trying to achieve together. It was missing.

A team that uses conflict avoidance to delay the discomfort of a challenging discussion hampers the team's growth and enables important issues to lie unaddressed. For example, if the 'team' mentioned earlier had been willing to address some of the critical issues, perhaps they might have come up with a solution whereby they formed two or more teams to address different tasks, producing a clear and compelling reason for working together. At a wider systems level, the team leader might have gained insight into how they led the group and reached a different perspective on how to group work tasks to form natural teams. Furthermore, those teams could have created more cohesive ways of working together and used different language to express the issues – away from relationships and personality and more towards process and task.

Conflict avoidance in teams can lead to frustration and foster a climate of the victim mindset. There is a stark difference between diplomacy in handling confronting situations and avoidance. Coaches are not immune from this either. Thinking about the previous example, years later, I acknowledge that we as coaches were probably complicit in helping the team avoid having the conversations they needed to have. Likely, we were also avoiding conflict too. Think back to a time when you avoided conflict – as a coach and as a team member.

You can use this simple activity in Table 4.2 to help the team have a conversation about avoiding conflict. Ask the team members to complete this individually and then to share it with the team. Follow-up questions might be:

- Based on what we've shared, what are the implications for how we work through challenges together?
- What are the implications for how unaddressed conflict might reduce our potential as a team?
- What might we need to pay attention to, e.g. how we are feeling about disagreements and conflict?
- How might we actively choose to step away from an issue – so that it's a choice, not a default position?
- What practices could we develop to navigate difficult conversations?
- How might we reflect on disagreements and conflict to draw out learning?
- Where might conflict show up for us as a team?

Table 4.2 Conflict Avoidance Self-Assessment

Times when I avoided conflict	What did I do – my behaviours?	What I was thinking – rationalising the situation?	What was I feeling – What was really happening for me?

Having simple agreements on how to channel conflict into a positive before it shows up is one reason for setting up the team agreements early in the relationship. Even without a team coach there, any team that does not have agreements about how they work together will eventually face a conflict situation. Better to be prepared than react to a situation in the heat of the moment.

4.3 Healthy debate to create

Optimising team potential means embracing chaos and potential conflict as an opportunity for creativity and is known as 'functional conflict'. For functional conflict to flourish, the team must have simple protocols in place to cover likely situations. For example, how the team will make decisions, and who will make them? Will there be protocols to deal with a stalemate? Yumi Stamet, working with self-organising teams in the health care sector, sums this up:

> [A]ny team that comes out of a conflict on the other end have been able to resolve it, they come out stronger.

Creative conflict is potential tension between ideas. In 2000, I was fortunate to visit IDEO offices in Palo Alto, California, as part of a development programme focusing on change. During the visit, I was intrigued by the office layout – bicycles hanging from the ceilings on a pulley system, a filing cabinet in the middle of the workspace full of 'failed' ideas for future reference. The lobby area was replete with products at various stages of their lifecycle. It was an Aladdin's cave of wonder and intrigue for a creative like me. But what struck me most was how they described their teams' ability to work together under intense time pressure and with differing skills and balance the 'chaos' that ensued. To experience this for yourself, check out a fantastic ABC News YouTube video (1999) for a masterclass to leverage healthy debate to create in the references section.

Harnessing conflict within the team for creative good is a core skill set for any team coach. We have already discussed contracting as a foundation for creative conflict. There are lessons to apply from organisations that do creative conflict well. Another colleague working in a holacratic self-organising environment puts this down to great feedback skills. Their organisation spent time and investment to train everyone in the skill of giving feedback. As coaches, we can role model feedback for the team and provide opportunities to develop further and nuance these skills.

In recent years, many organisations have invested in programmes designed to help people have difficult conversations. In the organisation where my colleague works, the ability to give feedback is essential for the smooth running of day-to-day operations. The driver for high-level feedback skills is multiple self-organising and self-determining teams. There is a real business purpose behind the skill of feedback. When we coach teams toward self-organisation, we're helping them discover for themselves the pros and cons of not giving feedback and creating productive protocols to do this, and asking questions about what team members are holding back on and exploring why is the first step to help the team define how to use the feedback.

> What was the best team you worked in? What were the key attributes that made it the best?

Coaching the team to embrace creative conflict takes time. The simple activity described here can start the conversation to help the team surface how they will harness the differences within the team. Ask each team member to jot down their thoughts about the best team they ever worked in. Ask them to think specifically about how the team used differences to achieve a creative solution or overcome a particular difficulty. The following attributes will likely appear somewhere on their list:

- The ability to have open discussion free from attachment to the idea being explored
- Willingness to listen deeply to others and change our minds if better ways of working emerged
- Embracing the discomfort of not knowing the solution because we knew together we would be able to work through it
- We listened to whoever in the team had the most expertise on the subject matter and trusted their expertise
- We were able to allocate tasks to sub-groups within the team and trusted people to do what was expected of them or let us know when they met a roadblock
- We built on each other's ideas
- We worked through things together

This activity creates a launchpad for a conversation about an experience of the best team and how this experience can be applied and utilised by their current team.

As a coach, it's useful for you to do this. Identify the best team you've coached for creating healthy debate to create. As you remember that team, think about how they worked through conflict. What you did to help them? What can you use to help the team you're coaching now be even better? If you're coaching the team as part of a co-coaching partnership, this is a great activity to do with your fellow coach. Together you can share ideas and identify approaches to use with the team to help them develop functional conflict. Understanding different perspectives is an excellent source for ideas and can help generate other options and is naturally where the conversation flows to create options and possible creative solutions and insights.

4.4   Mapping perspectives and perceptual positions

Mapping perspectives is an excellent way of helping a team understand different views on a particular topic within the group. Visual representation of perspectives can be beneficial to discover sources of conflict. The source of this activity is two-fold – one is perceptual positions used in therapy, based on the work of Virginia Satir and popularised within Neuro-Linguistic Programming. The other is mapping the forces for and forces against a particular topic created by Kurt Lewin in his group dynamics work. You can adapt both of these approaches to work with the team in a way that helps them understand the other person's perspective.

> As an aside, let us remind ourselves of our prime directive – to help the team self-organise and coach itself. Therefore, all of the activities outlined in the following intend to help the team move forward. In the perceptual positions activity, we discuss the conflict between team members. Naturally, the team only needs to consider this important if it impacts how the team works together to pursue its overarching task. As the coach, always check in – what is the impact of this on the team? What's the broader conversation we need to have together? We are not coaching individuals in the team but coaching the team as a collective. So contracting around the work to be done in service of the team is crucial before blithely spending time on an individual to individual conflict resolution. If there is no real impact on the team working together to achieve its goal – the issue is for individual team members to resolve outside the team sessions.
>
> If you are co-coaching the team, you might offer to coach the two individuals outside of the team coaching sessions. But these are separate from the team coaching assignment. In one organisation, I worked with both a co-coach and an individual coach who provided one-on-one sessions for individuals within the team. That way, we as team coaches avoided conflict of interest and were free from the content of the presenting individual conflicts.

Let us return to mapping out different perspectives. Start with identifying the point of contention and clarifying the real issue, for example, which method to use in a development activity, when to adopt a particular change and who has the final say on a piece of work. Whatever the topic might be, that becomes the focus of the forces that hinder progress or help progress. The team individually identifies what might be holding the team back from progress and what might help the team move forward – forces for and forces against. We are using this approach for working through conflict; therefore, it is helpful to ask each team member to do their version first. They can use sticky notes on a piece of flipchart paper, drawing a line down the middle and marking one side 'what's holding us back?' and the other side 'what's moving us forward?' for the chosen topic. When they've completed the activity, ask them to present each other about the forces for and forces against. It is likely that themes will emerge they can group, giving more profound insights into what might be behind the conflict at hand.

The next step is to understand how you might eliminate those things that are holding you back:

- What might you do to mitigate those forces?
- How might a resolution be made available?

Next, you review the positive forces:

- How might you amplify these?
- How might they be used to mitigate some of the negative forces?

Amplify the things that will move you forward, making them even more significant, stronger, louder, brighter and more concrete, and reducing or eliminating the things holding you back, so make smaller, make it into bite-sized chunks. How might you take each small item in turn?

This activity can take anything from 30 minutes to a couple of hours, and it is worth time-boxing the conversation. Explain what the activity is and ask the team how long they want to spend on the activity given the situation they're in and where they've reached. Regularly ask the group what's becoming more evident concerning what they're seeking to solve. Have a conversation with them as you work through this to find out how they're feeling, what thoughts or insights they're getting and what else they might need to do that they haven't done so far. Invite the team to get curious about the process and help them draw out their insights and learning. What are the questions the team needs to ask now concerning the conflict issue?

By the end of the conversation, not only will the team have understood and gained a deeper insight into the other's perspective, they will also have co-created a joint solution. There will be clarity on those things that are still unresolved. The team will have some steps on which they can move forward. As time goes by, they can agree on an action plan and who will do what. You can ask, what are you going to do with what you have learned? How will today's conversation help the team move forward? Asking questions that invite the team to consider how they use the conversation is part of the transition process we teach and creates a habit of team ownership. Any action the team commits to can be reviewed at subsequent sessions, either in or outside the coaching sessions. Team review outside of formal coaching is a sure sign of increasing team maturity. It signals that the transference process is starting, and the team is moving towards self-sustainment and organisation. Learning how to review progress after and apply the learning is a significant habit for a team to master and one at which high-performing teams excel. It is an opportunity for self-reliance and creates confidence for resolving future challenges they will face as a team. Questions that prompt discussion:

- How has this conversation helped you as a team?
- What will you do with what you've learned?
- What conversations will you have in future?

This approach is an excellent way of bringing issues to the surface safely, using the approach as a conduit for the conversation that needs to happen.

In one workshop with two different teams, we used the mapping tool towards the end of the session after having conversations about what the teams were looking to achieve together. The purpose of the activity was to gain an understanding of the other team's perspective. I asked them to explain the situation they were trying to work around from each team's perspective using the force field analysis. Mapping what was holding them back and what was moving them forward, I asked them to present their thoughts to each other. Two different teams were present – the project team and the delivery team. As they listened to each other's perspective on what was holding them back and what could move them forward, it became clear things were being said and heard for the first time. They could also start to see themes emerging around particular topics that were sticking points. Some of the same themes were shown as forces for by one team, whereas the other team showed them as forces against. Both teams realised they had a different perspective about what would resolve that sticking point. The mapping of perspectives started a conversation between the two teams. By the end of the session, they realised the straightforward activity of mapping perspectives enabled them to understand better where each other was coming from and a clearer line of sight on what was getting in the way of them working together. In a subsequent session, this activity had been a release point for more conversations and closer working.

Perceptual positions is a similar but different approach to gaining an understanding of another's perspective. As mentioned earlier, is it based on therapy and popularised in Neuro-Linguistic Programming co-created by Richard Bandler and John Grinder. However, its roots are in the psychotherapeutic field and came out of Virginia Satir's family therapy – most notably Parts Party. This helpful tool helps people understand another's perspective on the problem by inviting them to adopt the other's position. Taking the other's position means they take on the physiology and psychology of the other person by 'becoming' them in the conversation. This adoption of another's perspective has the benefit of allowing each other to better understanding the other's point of view.

Before working with the team using this approach, it is essential to check in with them and explore how safe they feel about working with this approach. If the conflict is with two individuals in the team, you could also explore using a goldfish bowl technique where the other team members watch from the outside what happens in the conversation. The title perceptual positions is significant because there are different levels of perception. I use four levels of perception because this brings in the system view of what is happening in the disagreement:

Level 1 – the person's view of their situation

Level 2 – the person's view of the other's situation from that person's perspective

Level 3 – the wider view of how the two people are interacting

Level 4 – the system view

The two people who have unresolved differing views would be in the centre, and everybody else would be observing from the edges. The observers would be in the fourth position giving input in the broader system view.

Ask the two people who are in conflict to explain their position – what they feel from their perspective is the root cause of the conflict and how they feel about the conflict. Once each has heard the other's perspective, ask them to swap physical position to where the other was standing or sitting physically. For example, Bob and Jill – ask Jill to switch seats with Bob and Bob to swap seats with Jill. Immediately, they have changed their physical position, which will likely impact their psychological position about the conflict. Ask them in this new position to assume the persona of the other – Bob becomes Jill and Jill becomes Bob. You ask Bob to talk as if he is Jill and explain the situation from Jill's perspective. Ensure he talks in the first person, so instead of saying 'Jill thinks . . . ', he says 'I think . . . ' relaying what he has heard Jill say about what she thinks as if he is she. Your role as the coach is to keep them in character, so if they start to say 'they' or 'she' or 'he', you bring them back and remind them that they are taking on the role of the other in this position. You would then ask Jill to explain how Bob feels from Bob's perspective. For example, Jill might say, 'I feel that Jill doesn't listen to me'. In this way, they take on the second perceptual position and explain what is going on in the conflict. In effect, they're having a dialogue with themselves as the two people. Instead of that dialogue being inside their head, it's verbalised in the real world.

Next, ask them to stand up or move away from where they were before and stand back and take a different perspective. This time ask them to take the observer's perspective:

- What did you notice about what was happening in that conversation?
- How did it feel to take on the persona of the other?
- What can you infer from this?

If the team participated in the activity, you invite them to offer their observations from a wider system perspective as the Super observers asking them:

- What did they notice about the observations Bob and Jill made?
- What did they notice about the interactions?
- What else might be happening here that neither Bob nor Jill is aware of?
- How might this be impacting the team that you were unaware of before?
- How might the wider system be influencing this conversation?

The team gains insight into the conflict with those two individuals and likely impacts the rest of the team. You can invite the team to debrief the activity. Ask them

- How has hearing the interaction helped the team?
- What are they as a team doing to contribute to this conflict?
- What is important for creating better ways of working?
- What might they be holding onto as a team that is amplifying the conflict?
- What will they do now?
- What is the question they need to answer together?

This example is one way you can use perceptual positions within the team between two team members.

The team will likely come in conflict with stakeholders outside of the team, and so you can do the same activity, but this time the team assumes the role of the stakeholder. Ask the team to put themselves in the position of the stakeholder:

- What's happening concerning the stakeholders and the team?
- How are the team and the stakeholders interacting?
- What's the relationship like?
- What's the world like from their position?
- What might each be feeling about the other?
- Think about the Physiology of the stakeholders. Where are they based?
- What kind of things are they challenged with?
- How might they be seeing what we're doing as a team?
- What are the data that they have on us as a team?
- What's really going on here in terms of the conflict?
- What's not being said?

Use the technique of the perceptual position as a mediator for the conversation, so you redirect the conversation in a way that creates another meta-level perceptual position. It takes the heat out of the discussion. You're using the technique to navigate that fiery path so that the team can have a more resourceful conversation.

When we're looking at conflict, it becomes an issue in teams because they have reached that stage where they can no longer reason. When we are no longer able to think rationally, we lose resourcefulness – we can't think about options because we get stuck in that track of our views and perspectives. When conflict happens in the world, it's usually because of a belief that has become embedded and means we are no longer basing any judgements on rational thinking. Instead, our decisions are based on a belief set.

Understanding conflict means entering the realm of beliefs. One of the other ways you can help the team understand their positions is by getting them to think about their beliefs. The way we talk about beliefs in organisations is assumptions. Beliefs can be a culturally loaded word when coaching teams, so if it becomes a trigger point for the team you're working with, take the heat out of the language and use a different word. Use the word assumptions.

- What are the underlying assumptions that we're making here that impact our ability to think in a way that will be productive?
- How might we have become tied to a particular assumption?
- What is getting in the way of our ability to make or create a way forward as a team?

Having a conversation about assumptions will likely start the team's thinking process of how they might be getting in their way. You can ask the team to think about other teams they interact with, especially if they are members of multiple teams. Bring in the learning from the wider team network to use as a resource for this team. You could ask them to bring examples of how those teams have worked through conflict and what might be helpful for this team and the current challenge. Ask them to think if they have seen this pattern of behaviours occur elsewhere in other teams, and how they coped with it, the methods they used to move forward. You can use different perspectives as a resource for the team to help them move forward. Ultimately, if the team is not in a position at that moment in time to move forward on the conflict, you need to take the stakeholders' perspective. Ask the team:

- How might the stakeholders respond to the fact that the team is not able to resolve this conflict?
- What might be the impact of this lack of movement forward on all stakeholders?
- What might the stakeholders have to say about this?

You could work with the team using the perceptual positions to bring in the stakeholder's voice by getting one of the team members to describe what the stakeholders might feel, think, say and see by role-playing the stakeholder. One technique I've noticed that works well, and you have to use this with care, and contract with the team, is to write the stakeholders names on pieces of paper and ask different team members to role-play that stakeholder. Each person sticks the piece of paper to their clothing so the rest of the team can see they are now stakeholder, Joe

Bloggs. Joe Bloggs is now part of the session, and the team can interact with him and ask questions. 'So Joe, what's your take on what's happening in the team at the moment?' 'How is it impacting you?' The team member that's assuming the role of Joe blogs explains the impact. If the team has data, for example, survey data, emails, any information and feedback of any description that has come in from Joe Bloggs, the person role-playing will use that data and bring it into the conversation. An even better version of this is to invite stakeholders to participate in the coaching session. Naturally, this will require careful preparation and agreement with both the team and the stakeholder(s) to set up the session for a productive conversation.

Perceptual positions and mapping perspectives are two of the perhaps most powerful tools to help teams work through any kind of conflict, disagreement or discussion sticking points that I've used. The beauty of these approaches is the simplicity, but that doesn't mean they're not sophisticated and nuanced. Sophistication also flows from how the session is set up. Ensuring that the climate is supportive, contracting or agreeing on how you will work together using the approach is key to its usefulness. When we use approaches that potentially explore what's in the mind of another, it requires heightened awareness, both team and coach, that anything might happen. I usually pre-frame with 'We're working here with what's happening inside our heads. We can't predict what might happen as we go through this approach. It's OK to call "time out" if you're feeling uncomfortable for whatever reason'. It's also worth challenging ourselves as coaches to check in and see how comfortable we are with what might come out. This method might not be an appropriate method for you or the team. Permit both you and the team to call time out and say, 'We're not ready for this yet'. If you are working with an individual outside of the team session, seek to understand what is going on individually. Have a conversation with the team about what is perhaps stopping the team from taking the conversation to a deeper level. Explore how safe they feel to have these types of conversations to discover what's preventing the team jointly. When using approaches that explore mental models, always do it with care – constantly observe what is happening. If you're co-coaching the team, make sure that the support coach is taking notice of subtle cues and check in regularly with each other to co-create a safe space for the team and coaches. Ultimately, being self-aware of your comfort level as a coach with whatever might come out of these types of conversations is essential.

I co-coached one of the tools similar to perceptual positions where we asked somebody to volunteer a scenario they wanted to work with. We carefully pre-framed the activity with 'Choose something that's not too complicated, too personal or too deep and meaningful. This activity is to demonstrate the approach, so you have a practical experience of using it'.

I was aware the approach might trigger something in the unconscious mind, so choosing something non-emotive and straightforward or complex helped create safety for the team and we as coaches. A volunteer stepped forward and offered a situation to work with. We asked the volunteer to choose people in the group to assume the roles of people in the case they wanted to work on. They labelled the roles and started the process. The volunteer began to direct the characters to act in a way consistent with the people in the case they'd chosen. We asked the volunteer to talk about the physiology of one of the characters – how might they be standing? How might they look in terms of facial expressions? And so on – through guiding the person who was role-playing this character. The volunteer suddenly became distressed. We stopped the activity to understand what was happening. We checked in with them to see if they were OK. They explained how the physiology question had triggered an emotional response because of the wider context of the situation they had chosen to practice. After exploring what this was about, we checked in to see if they wanted to end the activity. They were happy to carry on because they wanted to work through what was happening to gain insight.

Indeed, the client always brings you the real issue when they're ready. This person was prepared to have this conversation. The rest of the team were spooked by what had happened and weren't prepared to have the conversation. The debrief turned attention to the team to support them in what had happened and how they felt. We re-contracted how we would continue and helped create a safe space for the team to continue observing. In this case, it wasn't about helping the volunteer. It was helping the other team members cope with what had happened. Once we'd done the debrief and made sure everybody felt safe to carry on, we continued and completed the activity. At the end of the process, we checked in to see how everybody felt about what had happened. We debriefed the activity, the process and the value from the activity.

The key learning was that no matter how much we pre-frame, we cannot control what happens. People are unpredictable, and we cannot control what comes out in the moment. Sometimes we think it's about the individual who we were focusing on. In reality, the people observing are just as likely to be affected by what is happening. It's important to recognise this, especially in team conflicts – from mild disagreement to an out-and-out argument between two or more team members. Those people observing this happen will be as affected by it – albeit it in different ways. As coaches, we have to be aware of the protagonists; we also need to keep a peripheral awareness of the people sharing in the experience. Everything we do in the team environment influences the people around us. We exist in a 'quantum field', and we both affect and are affected by the people we work with.

This section on mapping perspectives and perceptual positions provides you with some ideas on coping with situations in the heat of the moment. You have these techniques and approaches ready and waiting to work with the team. The story given earlier is to help you understand how, as a coach, you can prepare yourself for any unpredictable situation that might occur. Develop a strategy you can fall back on when things go off the well-known track, and you're in the land of uncertainty.

You can stop any activity.

If you observe or hear something that tells you something is happening within the team – a pattern change in the team's behaviour, a behaviour that is puzzling you – call time out and check in with the team. 'Let's pause here. What's happening?' Ensure you agree with the team at the beginning of the relationship that you might use pauses or timeout to assist learning from time to time.

Pre-frame

Revisit the chapter on contracting and team agreements. Remember contacting happens all the time, and it's not something you only do once at the beginning of a team engagement. There are discreet and simple ways you can do this, 'I'm sensing the team wants to move into this area. Is everybody OK if we try something different?' This doesn't mean you're asking permission all the time because it could frustrate the team. Something as simple as 'How long should we spend on this activity?' helps you manage your inner state when a team is doing stuff that is unpredictable or something happens that you weren't expecting. This means you always have a fall-back process. Always pre-frame anything you do with the team in whatever way, shape or form that makes sense to you.

Debrief

Always debrief to allow learning and checking in with the team. The debrief is about the process and how people feel now having had the experience. Where are we now? What's helped so far? What has been helpful about the conversation so far? What has been unhelpful? Where are we going next?

Having a fall-back strategy in your back pocket means that no matter what comes up in the team coaching, you'll have a process for navigating the uncertainty. Conflict is highly unpredictable, and having some processes to help you support the team means it will feel less scary when it happens.

4.5   Chapter summary

Working with teams means that you will work with conflict sooner or later. Teams that thrive can debate and discuss different perspectives robustly and productively. Coaching teams who are in conflict tests our ability to work with our preferences for conflict and press on regardless. Ego-free coaching is required.

- Conflict is part of the human condition. Without it, we would never leave our comfort zones.
- Reframe how you think about conflict – see it as a spark of energy that can lead to creativity.
- Clarify the sources of conflict to establish potential options for resolution.
- Relationships aren't the only source of conflict, but we can help foster collective responsibility to produce more effective working relationships that allow for debate and foster ownership of outcomes.
- Help the team address the early stages of conflict before it escalates. If you must mediate the conversation, it's likely reached an escalation point already.
- Always remember that the coach is both part of the team system and separate from it. We must manage the boundaries between enabling the conversation versus rescuing the team.
- Contract around conflict early in the coaching process. Ask the team what it will do if it can't agree on something.
- Explore yours and the team's tendencies with conflict – do you/they avoid or welcome it?
- Cultivate feedback skills in the team through role modelling and giving the team opportunities to practice.
- Adopt approaches that provide learning opportunities for working through conflict.
- Perspective mapping and perceptual position are two approaches that might help team work through conflict.

Bibliography

ABC News Nightline. (1999) *Deep Dive – IDEO Build a Shopping Cart in 5 Days*. https://youtu.be/izjhx17NuSE. Accessed June 10, 2021.

Ernst, F. H. (1971) The OK Corral: The Grid for Get-on-With. *Transactional Analysis Bulletin*, vol. 1, no. 4, pp. 33–42. https://doi.org/10.1177/036215377100100409.

Gallo, A. (2017) *Harvard Business Review Guide to Dealing with Conflict*. Boston, MA: Harvard Business School Publishing Corporation.

Glasl, F. (2004) *Conflict Management: A Handbook for Managers and Consultants*, 8th updated and supplemented edition. Bern, Stuttgart, Vienna: Paul Haupt; Stuttgart: Free Spiritual Life Stuttgart, 2004, Figure 9.2: The 9 stages of conflict escalation, pp. 236–237 as well as Chapter 11: Interventions by Contact Treatment, pp. 313–347 (excerpts).

McLain Smith, D. (2008) *Divide or Conquer*. Portfolio Hardcover.

Stone Patton, H. (2010) *How to Discuss What Matters Most*. Penguin Publishing Group.

Thomas, J. (2000) *Glasl's 9-Stage Model of Conflict Escalation*. www.mediate.com/articles/ jordan.cfm##. Accessed June 10, 2021.

Van den Bos, K., Wilke, H., Lind, E., and Vermunt, R. (1998) Evaluating Outcomes by Means of the Fair Process Effect: Evidence for Different Processes in Fairness and Satisfaction Judgments. *Journal of Personality and Social Psychology*, vol. 74, no. 6, pp. 1493–1503. https://doi.org/10.1037/0022-3514.74.6.1493. Accessed June 11, 2021.

Chapter 5

Tools and techniques to aid the best thinking

Sustainability is the underlying premise of coaching self-organising teams. It's easy to fall into the trap of thinking tools are vital to creating sustainability. I guess that depends on what you mean by tools. This chapter offers you some different ways of thinking about tools and some traditional models to help create your own. What I share next might seem odd given that I've written several books on coaching tools, but tools are merely vehicles for enabling team mastery, and the team coach becomes the teacher of the coaching 'magic'. Therefore, before you start this chapter, remind yourself of the team coaching directive and the context you will use and create tools.

> The purpose of team coaching is to equip the team with the ability to become self-sustaining, able to coach itself and develop through continual deliberate or purposeful coaching practice.

With this in mind, let's take stock of our journey so far.

> How are we tracking?

This question is one of my favourite questions in any coaching conversation for two reasons:

1 It creates a natural pause in the conversation and allows time for people to think about what we've covered so far.
2 It's a great way of checking in and pausing. To see if the direction of travel is where the team wants to go. Another follow-up question – where do you think this is going? – creates the opportunity for the team to create another track!

DOI: 10.4324/9781003110583-6

In the previous chapters, we've spent time exploring team coaching and self-organising teams, how you can set up the team for success and some of the ways biases affect how teams and we work together. This discussion led to an exploration of how to handle disagreements and conflict. We're now going to consolidate some of the tools and techniques you can use to help teams do their best thinking, how they can develop and learn together to become self-sufficient.

5.1   Use coaching tools wisely

Typically, the notion of tools conjures up something structured and process driven with an end outcome in mind: something that you can follow step by step and you'll get a pre-determined outcome. If only coaching were that simple! In our book on coaching tools, Gillian and I explore how you can exapt, or re-purpose, and co-create tools to fit a situation. Think about how you might use these tools as you read through. I'd like you to imagine you've entered a magician's cave and you're standing in the entrance looking at the variety of different spells and magic books. Coaching tools are like a magic spell, and you can create anything you can imagine. And as you read that sentence, be aware this was a tool designed to evoke a different perspective about tools! Tools, therefore, can be magical, but if, like the Sorcerer's apprentice, you get too carried away and become enamoured of the creation process, chaos ensues. Coaching tools come with a health warning – use them with care and ensure that they are fit for purpose, they meet the context and as the coach, you are always free from attachment. Do not assume just because you've used a tool before in one situation that it's going to work in every case.

Your role is to help the team develop an explorer's mindset. Helping co-create space together because you never know what will come out of the conversation, you never know what the conversation might trigger, and you never know how individuals might respond to those triggers. There is always a possibility you co-create something utterly different from where you were starting. This possibility might open a door for the team to explore a separate room they didn't even know existed. The tools are the mechanism that opens the door of possibility.

This chapter aims to give you a framework and invitation to create your own tools. So you can work in the moment rather than being too prescriptive about how you work with the team. One team I worked with taught me a lesson about being emergent in the way I work as a coach and how coaching is more about being present than tools.

I went along to a team session fully prepared and thought, 'Okay, this is going to be a great session. I'm looking forward to it'. I had an idea of the tools we could use and how we could work together. When I arrived at the session, it was clear people were turning up with a less than positive mindset. Something had happened in the organisation. I was sensing all negative energy and noticed people weren't chatting and smiling – the air was quiet, and there were sullen expressions on most of the teams' faces. I said to them something like, 'I'm sensing something is going on that I'm not privy to. I'm noticing you're not as chatty as you normally are, and you seem a bit down. Tell me what's happening. What do we need to know about how we work together today?' They hesitantly started to explain what had happened. As they talked, more came out about how they felt – incredibly angry – about the situation and weren't feeling particularly positive towards the session.

I asked, 'So would it be helpful to explore some of that today rather than what we had planned? See where we go with that?' Naturally, they wanted to unpack what had happened, and I used a straightforward tool, brainstorming, to get everything 'out on the table'. 'Tell me what you're feeling now, what's going on in your head and let's just write that up on a flip chart just to get them out in the open'. We spent time jotting everything down free from interpretation or judgement, so we could see what was happening.

Once they had articulated everything, I asked the team to work out what they wanted to do. We looked at the list of things the team had mentioned and brainstormed what they wanted instead. Prefacing it with, 'What do we need to do in this session today that's going to be of help?' I asked each one to spend some quiet time first thinking about it and writing down their answers before sharing. Then, in turn, I asked each of them to share and put their thoughts on the flip chart choosing the top three things that would help. Using their ideas, the team developed a plan and decided who would do what and identify which things were outside of their control. So we used both a facilitation approach and process to help move the team forward.

Working with the team that day was not about necessarily resolving the issue. It was more about helping them process what had happened to them as a team. Sometimes there are no solutions or apparent solutions. The act of discussing and sense-making the situation is the work that needs to be done. Our coaching agreement, which we explore and discuss to gain learning, was a foundation value we held as we shared.

In a complex world, we cannot control what happens, and we need adaptability to work in the moment with what is presenting. An essential tool for all coaches is our ability to flex and sense when the team is not ready to have a conversation. Having tools or different approaches in your back pocket is essential if you are to stay present with the team and provide the help they need most when they need it. That doesn't mean you use them, but it gives you the confidence to coach, knowing they're there if you do. I could have taken the approach of helping the conversation without any need for activity. But it felt right to use a more facilitative approach based on what I already knew about the team. I've said this many times, but it's worth repeating. We are always using judgement in the interventions we take. Sometimes they create a productive result, and sometimes they don't. The key is the presence we bring to the room. Being present with the team is a tool.

> Hold lightly and never become attached to your tools. They are vehicles to aid discovery.

Coaching online or remote coaching has become the norm in the past year or so. The coaching world was already experimenting with virtual coaching sessions. My early coaching experience was almost exclusively on the telephone. I never met many of my coachees face to face. Therefore, the possibility of coaching teams online was exciting and presented many new opportunities. I enjoy coaching over Zoom and before that on Skype because it means I can work with clients worldwide. Having the world to coach is a great experience for working with different cultures. For some coaches, though, the online world can be confronting and leads to yet more challenges to overcome and one more thing to think about when we work with teams.

One of the challenges I often hear is how to read the energy of the team. Let's return to presence. Yes, it requires more concentration to conduct team coaching sessions online, and it is possible to sense the team mood by using acute observation skills and noticing pattern shifts. For example, maybe you are spotting a behaviour pattern change – perhaps in previous sessions, when team members turned up on the call, the team had been very chatty, laughing and so on. On this call, people are quiet, and there's not much interaction before the call starts. People turn up late, maybe don't have the cameras turned on. Whatever you observe is data; data are gold dust because you can use it to help the team understand what's happening and help you coach them towards that understanding. Perhaps the approach you and the team had planned for today isn't going to work.

Here are four categories of tools that have emerged throughout researching and writing this book:

- **The coaching process** – how we use the coaching process as a guide. I've designed the tools to help you think through your coaching process. Each coach will have their approach, so use them to help create your pathway to work with teams. Your experiences will be different from mine, and your process will reflect this. When you co-coach, it's helpful to share each other's coaching process so that you both can agree on which approach you will take.
- **Team growth and development** – understanding team maturity. It's helpful to know how well the team is working together and how long the team has worked together. Some approaches will work well with newly formed teams but will fall flat with a long-term team. The focus of attention will be

on enhancing and stretching and helping a mature team coach each other, whereas approaches with a new team will focus on co-creating how they'll work together.

- The third category is **team dynamics** – how you work with teams at the moment and help them understand the dynamics that are at play. Dynamics can include how they work through disagreements to how they leverage all the talents in the team. It can consist of how they relate to other stakeholders and how they interact with the wider organisational system.
- The final category is **universal** – any tools you can use in your team coaching, including creating your tools. It's important as a team coach to make your tools based on your learning as you work with different teams. Creating tools is an excellent way of developing your coaching skills and leveraging your maturity as a coach.

5.2   Foundational coaching tools

Before investigating the different tools, let's acknowledge three underpinning foundational tools that all coaches should have:

- The ability to ask powerful questions
- The ability to listen deeply to what is said and unsaid
- The ability to observe and give feedback in the moment in a way that is candid and helpful, and challenging.

Questioning

The ability to ask powerful questions is one of the core tools we have, yet it is often not seen as a tool. Over the years, I have amassed many different coaching questions keeping them in index card books. I have played with questions in co-coaching forums, picking questions at random to test them out on other coaches. Experimenting with different questions, getting feedback on their effectiveness and adding more to the collection have been helpful to me in so many different scenarios – not just coaching. Sometimes we overcomplicate coaching and look for the latest or greatest coaching tool when we have everything we need at our fingertips. It doesn't have to be sophisticated and fancy. It just needs to help the team!

Listening

This tool is an underplayed asset for all coaches. The ability to 'get' what and where the team is at means we must listen at a deep level. We must listen to what is happening in the room and what might be happening outside the room in the wider organisational system. If we are working as an external coach, our ability to stand back and be objective about what we hear is a tool for the team to use. This kind of listening requires us to be free from judgement and attachment. Listening at this level means we need to free ourselves from the tyranny of the commercial relationship we have with the organisation. We cannot truly listen if we are working on our agenda. For internal coaches, this can also be a challenge. Internal coaches are part of the organisational system and subject to many organisations' political and power influences. Objective listening is not an easy tool to use – it requires great skill and solid ethical boundaries.

Observation

Observation leads to feedback and challenge and is the third foundational tool. These three tools are linked because without deep listening, we cannot make observations, and without observations, we cannot ask powerful questions. Observation led feedback challenges the team's frame of thinking and mindset (assumptions).

Therefore, this chapter on tools is from the perspective that tools are methods of asking questions, listening for insights and giving observation-based feedback. All coaching tools will have these at their core, whether it's a questionnaire, a diagnostic or an activity – there will always be a question behind it, some element of listening and exploration, some element of observation and feedback regardless of the tool. Tools enable us (the team and the coach) to gain insight to move forward and take stock. We need feedback, and we need to be challenged. We need to understand and make sense as a team what we are learning and how we leverage that learning.

> Co-create tools with the team to leverage the power of collective brains working together.

Building on some of the tools created in Group Coaching (2013) and 50 Top Tools for Coaching (2019), I share some ways to develop your own tools and some of the core tools I have used in my practice to help teams. The format for these tools will be:

- The context
- Why use this tool?
- What is the tool?
- How to use the tool
- Self-reflection

The context

It is essential to understand this before developing the tool because you need to understand what situations this tool might apply. Not all tools suit all cases, and not all teams like the same kind of tools to work through a similar situation.

Judgement and awareness of the context in which you are working are essential before using any tool. Creating an agreement around experimentation is the first step in setting the context to help the team coach itself. A willingness to explore free from expectation is one of the core tenets of coaching teams.

Why use this tool?

Why use this tool versus any other tool? Why is this tool important in this context? Just because you have a tool does not mean you should use it. Sometimes, going back to the basics of questioning, listening and observation is enough. Coaching the team means self-coaching on being 'enough' and not trying to prove our value with an endless list of tools and activities. Both you and the team can become tool fatigued if you are not clear on why you are even using a tool.

What is the tool?

This section is an overview of the tool. It includes commentary on tool design and the hoped-for outcome from using the tool. Use an experimental approach to test the tool against your experience and update your learning about applying it in other coaching situations.

How to use the tool

The process steps described here are not prescriptive. As we have established, people are unpredictable, and you cannot allow for every variable in the way you construct a tool. Explore the process free from expectation and teach the team to do the same. If the process does not work the way intended, improve it, so it works for this team.

Self-reflection

The final section is an opportunity to capture your learning as you coach more and more teams. What worked and what did not, the situation you tested it in and so on. We talk later about reflection and how it is a great way to enhance the tools after each outing and make them your own.

5.3   Coaching process

Overall coaching process

The context

The coaching cycle is the overarching story for coaching the team. Figure 2.1 in Chapter 2 shows the overall coaching cycle. The coaching process is the sub-plot within the story and is how you will work with the team from the moment you engage with the organisation. If you are working as an internal coach, your entry point is when you are assigned to the team as their coach.

Why use this tool?

The process is an important place to start because it provides a framework for you to follow. That said, it is not rigid. Think of it more as a guide to help you and save cognitive overload to give you a pathway. It will help you educate the organisation on what you'll be doing with the team and provide some certainty about the team coaching process. Bear in mind that the team will potentially feel uncomfortable or uncertain. A process helps create enough certainty. Remember that our role is to co-create, and as you discover more about the organisational system, you can flex your process to suit. There is no magic wand, and a flexible approach demonstrates co-creation from the outset.

What is the tool?

I've purposely used a circular flow for the process rather than linear boxes because although some steps happen sequentially, the first session always comes first. There might be repeated activities over and over within each session.

There are similar activities that could happen at any stage in the process; hence, they fall in the middle of the circle.

How to use the tool

The entry point is where we start the process. This terminology identifies the type of role you are likely to adopt at this stage in the coaching, which is more of a consultancy approach. The next step is to explore, and this is where you find out who the team members are, what the work is likely to be and any assumptions. It is the stage at which you might form hypotheses or points of view about the team and the organisational system, including stakeholders. You might also think of this as the empathy phase as you develop a deeper understanding of the system. We bring in lean startup and design thinking techniques and tools to our practice; hence, we think of it as the empathy phase. So we want to empathise with the team and the system in which we're working.

As we cycle through the process, we become more informed, and the activities within each step develop based on that feedback. Our hypotheses might also change as we deepen our knowledge of the team and the organisation. See Figure 5.1 for the process cycle and explanation of the activities.

Guidance notes

Assess the process against your own experiences. If you're new to coaching teams, find a team to practice with and develop your own process that makes sense to you.

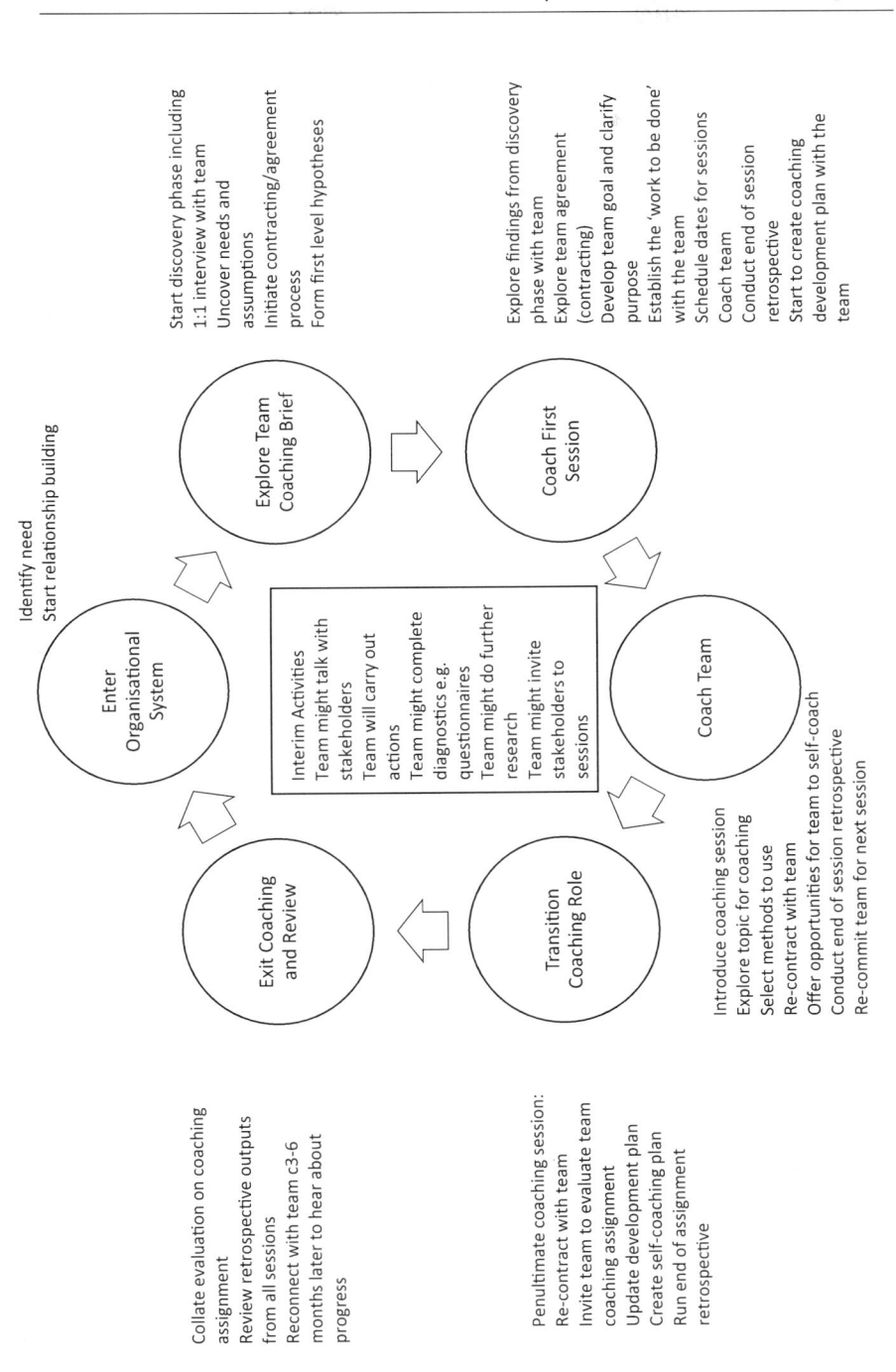

Figure 5.1 Iterative Coaching Process

Self-reflection

I cannot overemphasise the importance of using this as a framework to guide your practice. I sometimes add more steps, introduce different approaches, remove activities and add new ones. I always have in mind the plan, do, check, act cycle flowing through the synapses. Context, remember, is a defining factor. No two teams in the same organisation behave in the same way. Therefore, take an experimental approach and remain open to new ways of thinking and doing. Experimentation is crucial, which also requires ego-free coaching.

Consider how you could create a flexible process and how you would review its usefulness.

Contracting

The context

In Gorell (2013), I talk about contracting in the context of group coaching and compare it with trying to solve the Rubik's cube – trying to get all the colours to line up in three dimensions is a good analogy for contracting

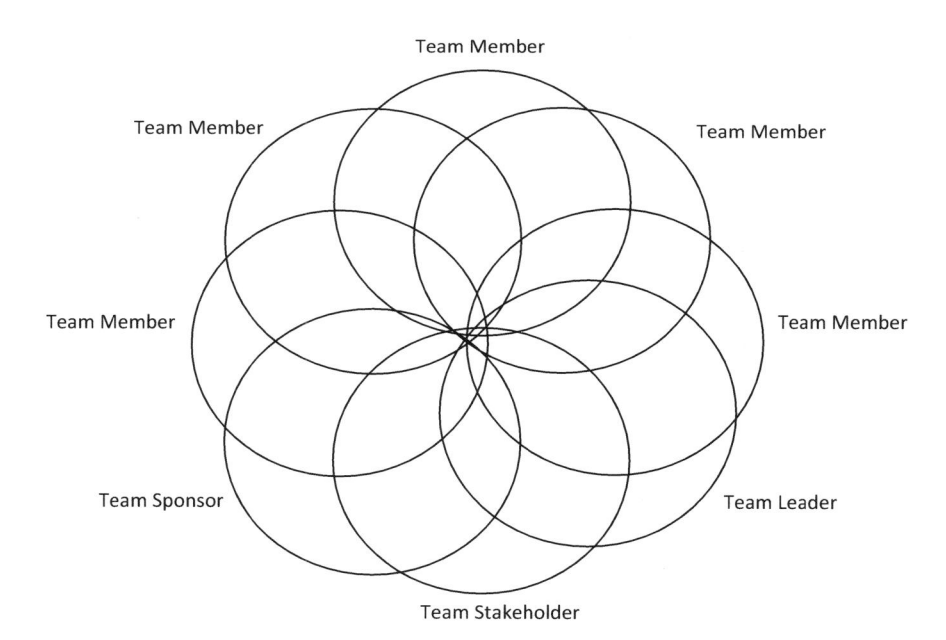

Figure 5.2 Contracting in Complex Systems

Adapted from Group Coaching, Ro Gorell (2013) with permission from Kogan Page Ltd with multiple stakeholders in a complex environment. Creating agreements in team coaching is equally complex because the process aims to reach an agreement with all interested parties. Although the Rubik's cube is a complicated puzzle rather than complex, i.e. it can be solved once you understand the technique, whereas contracting with teams is an ongoing puzzle with no obvious solution.

The details of the contracting process will vary depending on the organisational model, e.g. hierarchical, holacratic, etc. In a hierarchical system, there is likely one key sponsor for the team. Therefore, this person is included in the contracting phase and the individual team members, team manager or leader. In self-organising teams, the team manager or leader role will likely change as they could be transitioning from manager to coach. Other key stakeholders will be included in the contracting process, particularly if they directly impact or are impacted by the team's work.

In a holacratic organisation, the organisational system becomes part of the contracting process. What are the enabling constraints the organisation places on the teams and how they work within it? In Chapter 2, we investigated some of the enabling constraints in Figure 2.1.

Contracting is a never-ending process – everything in the coaching arena is with agreement.

Why use this tool?

There are many tools for creating agreements. Here I invite you to think about how you might use different approaches for making agreements with diverse stakeholders – rather than having one tool to rule them all!

What is the tool?

The contracting process starts from the moment you first engage with the organisation about coaching the team. The questions you ask at the discovery phase informs what each of you expects from the other and how you will work together. The process is like a continual dance where you expand your understanding of the relationship with each step – retracing and rephrasing how the connection is working. The first session with the team continues and develops the conversation and agreement process.

This tool is more of a guide to enable emergence and support the team in constructing an agreement informed by discussion. I am grateful to Liz Keogh for her inspiration and the use of 'dyads' in framing conversations in complex systems.

As you continue to work with the team, you can use this simple guide to provide an enabling constraint for working together. This guide is helpful as a container for the conversation on how you will collaborate in a productive and meaningful way.

How to use the tool

Harness the data you have gathered from the discovery phase and use this data to create some conversation triggers. Create a continuum with two positive yet opposite statements. Ask each team member to self-assess how they would like the team to work together around these continua. Either use an online tool or ask individuals to write their assessments individually before plotting on a larger piece of paper. In this way, you will avoid groupthink. Use these assessments as a starting point for discussion.

Encourage team members to support their assessment with an example. As you move through the continua, ask the team to synthesise what they've discussed into some fundamental principles for how you and the team will work together. Encouraging discussion that leads to the creation of principles allows for emergent thinking and means you avoid the standard 'ground rules' approach to contracting. See Figure 5.3 for some examples.

Self-reflection

How might you review how they team is working with you and how they're working together as a team? How do your needs and wants as the coach or coaches map into this process? How might you introduce the concept of an integrated complex system to support this conversation and use it as an education piece? Could you perhaps include conversations about what has worked well with other teams they've been part of and what has not worked so well? How might they build on the things that worked and reduce the likelihood of the things that didn't work cropping up in this team?

Session planning

The context

Every session will be different. That said, it's great to have a compass to guide you. Arriving at a team coaching session with a blank page can seem daunting to

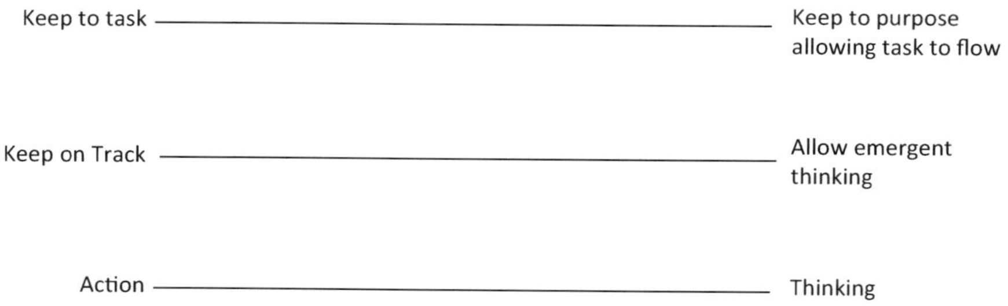

Keep to task ———————————————— Keep to purpose
allowing task to flow

Keep on Track ———————————————— Allow emergent
thinking

Action ———————————————— Thinking

Figure 5.3 Contracting Using Emergent Conversation

some. This tool is offered to help you create a cadence of connecting with teams and introducing the sessions.

Why use this tool?

A strong start is always helpful and creates confidence in the coach from the beginning of the relationship. Typically, the sessions will last anywhere between two and four hours. Online sessions are at the lower end of that range.

We always create a session plan for all interventions – training, coaching, mentoring and meetings. Sometimes we co-create them on the fly, usually where we have a deeper level of trust with the client. Regardless, it's always helpful to have something to refer to. We use a session plan as a launchpad to know how we'll start the session. Getting off to a good start means we can freewheel wherever the session takes us. It's unlikely that the session flows precisely according to the session plan. Remember that no plan survives first contact with the customer!

What is the tool?

A simple framework helps you channel your thoughts into a flow that will help frame the conversation and enables you to visualise timeframes. Framing the conversations into outcomes helps elicit the reason why. Why is this an important topic for the team?

See Table 5.1 for a sample session plan.

Table 5.1 Session Plan – Example First Session

Team Coaching First Session

Time	Topic, Goal and Purpose	Outputs and Outcomes	Activity
Session Timing Three Hours			
00:00–00:10	1. **Welcome & introduction and scene setting** Goal: context setting, why we're here	Outcomes: The team gains clarity on why they're here	Context for session – team members
00:10–00:25	2. **Check-in** Goal: hear from everyone in the room	Outcome: everyone's voice heard in the room	Quick round the room using a check-in question
00:25–00:45	3. **Introduction to team coaching** Goal: get everyone on the same page	Outcomes: agreement on the way forward. Sense of achievement and know what the next first steps are	Introduce core concepts and allow for brief Q&A session Role of coach Role of team members

(Continued)

Table 5.1 (Continued)

Team Coaching First Session

Time	Topic, Goal and Purpose	Outputs and Outcomes	Activity
00:45 –01:15	**4. How we'll work together** Goal: get initial thoughts about how to create a safe learning space	Outputs: populated first part of team canvas Outcomes: everyone feels safe being themselves. We know how we'll work together	Populate team canvas and have a meaningful discussion about likely barriers and enablers working together in an exploratory and emergent way
01:15–01:45	**5. Share core themes from the discovery phase** Goal: explore the work to be done by the team	Outputs: discussion Outcomes: clarity on the areas the team wishes to work on	Possibly use Jamboard/flipchart to collate core themes?
01:45–01:55	BREAK		
01:55–02:40	**6. Creating team goal and purpose** Goal: discuss the team's goal and purpose to gain alignment or reveal misalignment	Outputs: populated second part of team canvas Outcomes: everyone is clear on the purpose and goal for the team coaching and accepts this may well emerge differently as we work together	Update the team canvas with purpose and goal and discuss complex adaptive systems, i.e. the emergence of goal as we journey through Identify some key success measures that provide direction without being too prescriptive
02:40–02:45	**7. Evaluation** Goal: to encourage learning team and create learning habit of reflection	Outputs: Chatbox what they'll stop, start and continue Outcomes: everyone shares their learning	What will the team STOP|START| CONTINUE
02:45–03:00	**8. Wrap up and team retrospective** Goal: identify what has emerged from the session and what they appreciated about working with each other	Outcomes: the team learns gratitude for what is already working in the team	Appreciation of each other's input and commitment to attend next sessions

How to use the tool

Create a table in word document using the headings suggested in Table 5.1. The topics and activities in the example are only suggestions. Naturally, once you have gone through a discovery process with the team, you will identify the real topics the team wants to focus on and have identified topics that might be useful to help the team develop their coaching nous.

Self-reflection

How might you co-create session plans in the session itself? Having this framework means you could create a blank template to engage the team in developing their own, or you could invite the team to develop their own from scratch.

Discovery questions

The context

Developing relationships with team members and stakeholders start from the very first meeting. If you work as an internal coach, this is when you are assigned to a team. Suppose you're external it's when your prospective client has the first conversation. In the discovery phase of coaching, every conversation adds to our understanding of the context and how we can help the client. Specifically, you will likely conduct one-on-one discussions with all team members and key stakeholders before formally coaching the team.

Why use this tool?

Formulating questions that will help understand the organisational context within which the team works, and the team climate is essential. It provides information on which you can develop working hypotheses and an indicator of the likely first steps you might take with a team.

Second, it's a great way to start to build trust with team members. During the coaching sessions, you will work with the team as a collective. The discovery conversations are an opportunity to create relationships with each team member. And gain insights about how they would like to work with you within the team.

It is both an information gathering and a trust-building activity.

What is the tool?

It is a set of questions for you to consider when conducting the one-on-one sessions. The questions are not fixed. They will change as you realise which aspects of the team context you need to understand.

How to use the tool

The tool invites you to think deeply about which questions make sense for this particular team and context. What do you need to know to work well with this team? The questions suggested in Table 5.2 are based on some of the questions used over the years. The order of the questions might make sense, or they might not.

Over the years, I have found that having just a handful of questions helps the conversation flow. Asking the same questions of each team member and stakeholder means you can compare and contrast answers to see if themes emerge.

The aim here is not to diagnose the team's problems but to provide themes the team can reflect on and make sense for themselves.

Table 5.2 Discovery Questions Questions Bank – Work out your strategy first before you decide which questions to ask. Adapt the questions for stakeholders, e.g. what are one or two challenges from your perspective that this team is facing?

How long have you been with the team?

Describe how you see yourself within this team?

What are your main barriers to doing your best within this team?

What might the challenges in how the team self-organises?

What is the team's main goal?

How aligned are you with the team's main goal?

How does decision making currently work in this team?

How much do you need each to achieve your goal?

Tell me, what is going well in this team?

What is this team good at?

What is this team not good at?

If you were an outsider looking at this team, what are the key nuggets you would offer to help them develop their effectiveness?

What are the one or two most significant challenges the team is facing short, medium and long term?

How do you experience communication within the team?

What observations do you make about role clarity within the team?

How do you see team coaching helping with the overall objectives of your organisation?

How would you like to work with me/us as your coach/coaches?

What is not going so well in this team?

Who are the key stakeholders for this team?

Describe your dream team?

What does your team aspire to be?

What would make coaching worthwhile for this team?

What would make coaching this team worthwhile for the organisation?

How do you want this team to leave a legacy to the organisation?

If you had complete freedom, what would your agenda be for this team?

This is where the contracting process begins – and informs the team about how they work together in the coaching space.

Self-reflection

Sometimes putting yourself in the shoes of your coachees helps identify the relevant questions to ask. Ask yourself, if you were a member of this team, what questions would you like to be asked? Challenges and issues can usually be turned into questions, so think through some of the core challenges and questions teams face, particularly when they're self-organising and turn these challenges into questions?

Keep questions high level and focused on establishing the context in which you're coaching the team.

5.4   Team growth and development

Creating safety

The context

Helping the team create and maintain psychological safety enables learning and development. It also provides a bedrock of constructive conflict. A team must have the capability to have disagreements and still function well as a team. Edmondson's questions provide a great starting point and opportunity to explore where the team is and how they can move forward together to create a safe environment to grow.

Why use this tool?

This tool provides an opportunity for discussion and conversation. Introducing the concept and enabling the team to have a free flow conversation mean creating safety by having the conversation.

What is the tool?

This is an educational tool – the coach takes on the role of educator/trainer bringing the concept, theory and questions so the team can discuss and use as a conversation starter for how the team sits concerning psychological safety. The coach/es must read Edmondson (1999) to understand the concept to help the team explore in more detail what it means.

How to use the tool

The coach describes psychological safety, outlines the questions and invites the team to explore the questions. How the team uses the questions will vary. Perhaps they might wish to consider them individually first, or collectively.

Table 5.3 A Survey Measure of Psychological Safety

1. If you make a mistake on this team, it is often held against you (R)
2. Members of this team are able to bring up problems and tough issues
3. People on this team sometimes reject others for being different (R)
4. It is safe to take a risk on this team
5. It is difficult to ask other members of this team for help (R)
6. No one on this team would deliberately act in a way that undermines my efforts
7. Working with members of this team, my unique skills and talents are valued and utilised

Source: Copyright Amy Edmondson, The Fearless Organisation Figure 2.1 Used with Permission.

How the team works together can be an interesting point of discussion when the team reviews the session. For example, if answered individually first, versus discussing the questions collectively, what does this suggest about psychological safety within the team?

Self-reflection

How safe do you feel within the team as the coach/coaches? Would this be an interesting topic to discuss with the team? What might this mean for how you contract and re-contract with the team?

Team process review

The context

Helping the team make explicit how they work together creates an opportunity for developing team protocols. This tool provides a framework for team members to notice what is happening and discuss what works and doesn't. It is useful to introduce this early in the coaching assignment and create the team development plan.

Why use this tool?

Having a tangible way of describing behaviours and working practices makes it easier to identify problem areas and improvements. It takes the conversation from a theoretical to a practical level. It also helps create the habit of review and retrospective, so the team continually learns.

What is the tool?

It is a simple set of questions grouped around themes. Individual team members notice behaviours and can jot down their observations.

How to use the tool

Introduce the tool as a way of observing and learning what is happening in the team. Allow the team to practice using it for a specific activity first to experience how they might use it. Review their observations and invite them to use this tool to learn and develop working practices.

Team members take notes as they observe each other's behaviours against the core activities identified, e.g. initiating, asking, etc. See Table 5.4 for example areas. The team can add their own. These are suggestions to get you started. I have populated one name with a couple of examples to show you how this might look.

Self-reflection

How might this tool work in real life? We don't often take stock of how we do everyday things at work. How might you combine this tool with a retrospective activity?

5.5 Team dynamics

Identifying sources of conflict

The context

Teams often get hung up on conflict and attribute it to relationship issues. Relationships become the catch-all for the conflict and disguise the actual source. This catch-all leads teams to go off at a tangent. Having a conversation starter that increases productive conversations helps.

Why use this tool?

It provides a visual aid to thinking and focuses the team on identifying the source of the presenting issue. Conflict can sometimes lead to a downward spiral, and this tool focuses the team's attention outside of their world and on a different perspective.

What is the tool?

The tool is based on the Ishikawa diagram or fishbone. The presenting conflict is the head of the fish, and the bones are the sources of the conflict.

How to use the tool

We move in and out of coaching and facilitating with this tool. Initially, you will facilitate the process and gradually step away, asking the team to pause at specific key

Table 5.4 Team Process Review – With Example

Team member	Initiates • Proposes • Ideas • Suggests • Clarifies points raised	Asks • For information • For other's ideas and opinions • For suggestions • For proposals • What others want	Offers • Information • Ideas • Suggestions • Thoughts • Points of view	Describes • Builds on others' ideas • Explores ideas • Clarifies points made	Summarises • Explains in their own words what they've heard • Paraphrases what others have said • Mirrors back what they've heard	Decisions • Asks the team for a decision • Offers a decision for the team	Supports • Praises and acknowledges other team members' contributions
Joe Bloggs	Joe initiated a conversation about ABC topic			Joe built on Prina's idea about introducing prototyping XYZ product in a live environment			
Team member name							
Team member name							
Team member name							
Team member name							
Team member name							
Team member name							
Team member name							

learning points that you observe as the team works together. You might, for example, ask 'what is important now about resolving this conflict?' if you hear the team are having moments of insight or realisation. Remind the team they own this and be prepared that resolution might not be forthcoming in one session. The team might have to regroup and find more data or reflect on the conversation before concluding.

Begin the process by drawing a fishbone diagram using Figure 5.4 as an example.

Invite one of the team to write up a summary of the conflict they're seeking to resolve. It may be the team spends time discussing this before they come up with a summary statement.

Invite the team to add the bones to the fish and discuss the possible sources of the conflict. It could be a process, or resources, or skills or goals. It's helpful to invite the team to brainstorm what the bones of the fish might be, so they own the perspective of the problem. Whilst I have given examples here, hold off giving these to the team and let them come up with their own.

Once the bones are labelled, the team can start to ask the '5 Whys'. Why is process an issue?

This is a simple tool the team can use themselves – having set up the concept. You can go into full coach mode. The team has an opportunity to work together in a self-organised way, and your role is to be the team's conscience. Asking the team to review what's happening in the room? Where are they now in their thinking? How are they feeling? What might happen if they leave today without a resolution? How might the team move forward? These questions are non-contextual ideas to get you started. Naturally, when you are in the room with the team, the questions will become apparent based on what you are seeing, hearing and experiencing.

Self-reflection

How might you feel about letting go of the facilitation process? What might you contribute to help the team? How can you be present in the team system yet remain objective? How might your contract with the team for how you work together on this activity? What additional ground rules might you need?

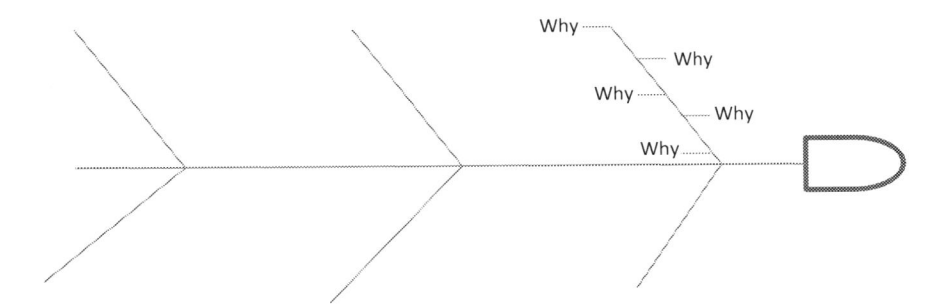

Figure 5.4 Fishbone and 5 Whys

RACI matrix

The context

One potential source of conflict within teams is a lack of clarity around role and responsibility. In the example from Buurtzorg in Chapter 7, teams have crystal clear clarity on who is doing what and why. Prescribing roles and responsibilities early in the team formation process ensures that there is no overlap on tasks.

As with any tool, you need to be guided by the team about what is helpful. It is likely during the discovery phase to see a theme around roles and responsibilities but not always the case. The first session is about understanding what you will work on with the team.

Why use this tool?

This tool helps frame a conversation about who does what with the team and why. In team coaching, we specifically want to understand how not having clarity impacts the team's ability to perform.

What is the tool?

The tool is a matrix of all the roles both within and peripheral to the team, so everyone understands each role:

- Who is responsible – they are tasked with completing the activity (R)
- Who is accountable – they ultimately own the decision (A)
- Who is consulted – they have a stake in the outcome of the activity (C)
- Who is informed – they have a peripheral interest but are not impacted directly by the activity (I)

How to use the tool

This tool can be introduced by the coach – using a facilitation stance explains the process and then steps away and allows the team to self-organise. Draw the matrix in Table 5.5 that explains the different categories of R A C I.

Invite the team to discuss all the roles and identify the categories for each role. The role names of the key stakeholders are on the top of the matrix. Ask the team to populate this.

Taking a coaching stance, ask the team questions such as

- What impact is not having role clarity having on the team's performance?
- How might this help you perform as a team?
- What do you notice about the conversations you're having now?
- What questions do you need to ask your stakeholders?

Table 5.5 RACI Matrix

RACI Matrix				
Activity	Roles			
	Team Sponsor	Team Member	Role	Role
For example, payroll				
For example, annual leave				
For example, shift swaps				

Self-reflection

How might you introduce this tool if the team has spotted a lack of clarity around roles and responsibilities? What stance will you take, e.g. educator, facilitator, coach or consultant? What role does the team need from you? Where do you feel most comfortable?

5.6   Universal tools

Tool creation

The context

Tools are instruments to help you help the team. In the last 13 years, I've lost track of how many tools I have created. Keeping your toolkit fresh is vital in a complex world. The ability to adapt and the exaptation of your coaching practices ensures that you stay alert to changes in your environment and you are best positioned to help the teams you serve.

It's important not to tie yourself to a particular framework or tool because we want the ability to meet the team where it's at and reduce the bias we'll bring naturally to the coaching scenario. Adopting a beginner's mind is always helpful when developing tools. We can also iterate tools based on what we experience, for example, adding questions to our questions bank for the discovery phase because we find something works well or by adapting a different approach to our coaching process.

Why use this tool?

Experimenting with co-creation is a helpful approach to creating tools for yourself. Each time you use a tool, you'll be co-creating something that is contextually relevant and has meaning for the team you're serving.

Creating your tools for coaching teams means you'll also increase your confidence, and the reliance on tools will diminish. It's a paradox that I rarely rely on tools in coaching conversations. However, if needed, I can draw on my toolkit and create tools with the team as we're talking. Often the source of the tool comes from the team. I become the conduit for their ideas and provide a framework to assist them.

What is the tool?

There are some simple aids for creating tools, and once you realise this, you'll be able to develop tools with the team in real time. In Jones and Gorell (2021), this is one of the tools we describe.

Here are the four different approaches to creating tools. You have seen some of them throughout this book.

How to use the tool

The categories of tools give you a template to develop your own tool. These simple formats allow you to create multiple tools and are easy to remember so that you can develop tools on the fly. For example, in one session, I used a 2×2 matrix to describe how people might respond to change. The team asked lots of questions about stakeholders and resistance, and it occurred to me that a simple visual might help the conversation. I used the X-axis to map readiness for change and the Y-axis to map willingness to change. This led to a discussion about where people in the organisation might sit concerning these categories and the implications for them in their team.

The continuum type tool is helpful in mapping extremes of a topic. There is an example of this in Figure 3.2 of Chapter 3. I have used this type of tool many times. It's a great way of synthesising conversations and creating opposites. This mapping activity creates two kinds of conversations: one that clarifies the opposite ends of the spectrum. The other assesses the current reality. I have also used this to share information. For example, you could create a continuum for psychological safety and ask the team to identify what each end of the spectrum might look like for the previously mentioned seven key questions. The possibilities are endless.

The prioritisation ladder can be used in combination with perspectives mapping. For example, the team can list all of the factors holding back and supporting the situation. The next step is to prioritise them using a ladder. In this situation, all of the opposing forces would be on one side of the ladder and the positive forces would be on the other side.

The radar or wheel tool is helpful to compare different factors and score on a scale of 1–10. For example, you could use this tool to collate the themes from the discovery process and ask the team to rate from 1 to 10. Ask them to assess where they would like to be on a scale of 1–10, where 10 is fully satisfied. Then ask them to rate in a different colour where they are now concerning that theme. Ask them to discuss what they did to get to their current score. Then using a

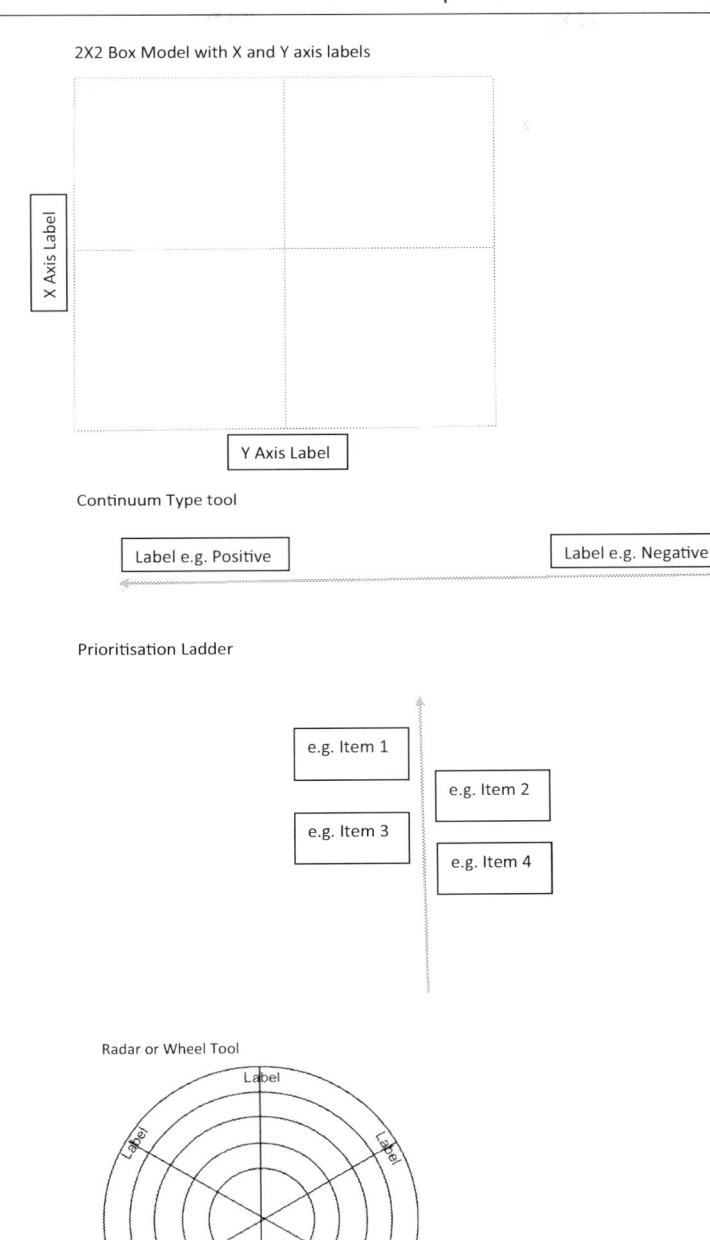

Figure 5.5 Tool Categories

Source: From 50 Top Tools for Coaching, Gillian Jones, and Ro Gorell (2019) Reproduced with permission from Kogan Page Ltd

solution-focused approach, ask if they went to bed tonight and supposing a miracle happened. Overnight that theme had been resolved. When they wake up the following day, what's the first thing they notice?

Self-reflection

Take note of how you use the tools – what worked? What didn't work? What feedback did you get? What did you notice about how the team perhaps adapted it themselves? How might you adapt the tools? Keep different versions of the tools in a toolkit on your computer, and soon you will have hundreds that you've created to use and adapt in any situation.

5.7   Chapter summary

How you work with a team and the tools you use will be different each time. You can create a set of tools to have at your disposal and, even better, co-create tools with the team. The co-creation process is another opportunity to transfer skills and knowledge to the team, so you leave them in an even better place at the end of the coaching assignment.

- Coaching tools are merely vehicles through which you enable team mastery.
- Use coaching tools with care and ensure that they fit the context. Be vigilant about your habits of relying on a small set of over-used tools and stay unattached. Your favourite tools might not suit the team or context.
- The team chooses what help they need. Tools might be appropriate or not. Focus on the conversation first and use tools to help dig deeper into topics.
- Four categories of tools to consider

  - The coaching process
  - Team growth and development
  - Team dynamics
  - Universal tools

- Three tools coaches have yet they don't classify them as tools:

  - The ability to ask powerful questions
  - The ability to listen deeply to what is said and unsaid
  - The ability to observe and give feedback that is candid and helpful.

Bibliography

Edmondson, A. (1999) *The Fearless Organisation.* Hoboken, NJ: Wiley.

Gorell, R. (2013) *Group Coaching; A Practical Guide to Optimizing Talent in Any Organization.* London: Kogan Page.

Jones, G., and Gorell, R. (2021) *50 Top Tools for Coaching: A Complete Toolkit for Developing and Empowering People*, 5th edition. London: Kogan Page.

Chapter 6

How to cope with change – creating fearless learners

Helping teams cope with change is an increasingly important aspect of our coaching toolkit. As we move through the continuing challenges of the COVID-19 pandemic, organisations, governments and communities realise that our world has changed significantly. Technological changes were already increasing the pace of change, and the global pandemic accelerated this type of change and threw social and political challenges into the mix. Now, more than ever, we must help teams develop a flexible and helpful coping strategy to traverse both incremental and life-altering change.

What does this mean in the world of work? How can we help teams cope with change and see it as necessary to thrive during uncertainty and navigate complexity?

We explore these questions in this chapter and focus on three topics – the nature of change, how we can help teams navigate the paradox of control and going with the flow. The third topic is perhaps one of the most popularised models of personal change – the Growth Mindset. Here I present a different perspective on the model and interweave the concepts of change and individual versus systemic change.

6.1 Change – what is it?

You and the team will likely have experienced a lot of organisational change. There are many models, methods, theories and myths around organisational change. In fact, over the last 20 years, tools, models and techniques have overwhelmed organisations. Consultants provide their models and methods that provide 'the answer' to the latest challenge. It's easy, therefore, to forget what we mean when we talk about change. In simple terms, change is a move from the status quo. The dictionary definition gives us 'replace something with something else that is newer or better'. In business terms, this can be anything from a process, software, business model, organisation structure, roles and so on to a complete pivot of a business identity.

The 'C' word can often strike fear or anxiety in teams and individuals within. Organisations grapple with balancing the need to increase performance whilst maintaining business as usual. There is an inherent paradox in managing

DOI: 10.4324/9781003110583-7

change – maintaining the status quo to deliver customer outcomes yet introducing a new status quo to improve or make more efficient an existing activity. Change is an integral aspect of being human – our cells die off and replace all the time without us consciously being aware of it. In essence, we are designed for change. What is it about change that has made it such a focus of attention in the world of work?

What if we were to think of change in three ways: transactional, transitional and transformational?

Helping teams cope with change starts with clarifying the type of change the team is working on or how they are affected by the change. To help start the conversation, Figure 6.1 can act as a catalyst for the discussion and describe the change in simple to understand terms.

Often when organisations embark on change, they use 'management speak' that makes it challenging to have meaningful conversations about 'so what is it exactly?' As part of the agreement phase in a recent session, one of the things the group wanted from me was 'no fancy words'.

Starting with questions helps the team and often surfaces assumptions about the change and gaps in the team's understanding and organisational gaps. For example, using this simple thinking process of transactional, transitional and transformational can help clarify questions about strategy and direction and help the team understand where they have agency. A topic we will return to later.

> What is the type of change?
> What is the direction of travel for this change?
> What are our assumptions about the change?
> What are the natural boundaries for this change?
> What are the constraints for this change?
> What might be the unintended consequences of this change for – team, process, tools, resources, etc.?
> How much change have you experienced as a team in the last year?
> How might your previous experience colour your assumptions about the present change?

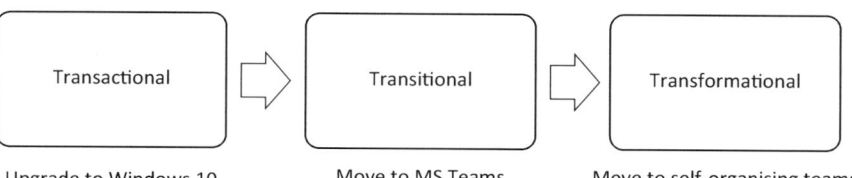

Upgrade to Windows 10   Move to MS Teams   Move to self-organising teams

Figure 6.1 Three Types of Change

The following is to help you as the coach describe the model and start the conversation.

Transactional

Physical changes to I.T. systems and processes, for example, are tangible kinds of change. These are what I call transactional types of change. They might have implications for teams and their members, yet they are, on the whole, tangible and easy to name. See Figure 6.1 for an example of this.

Transitional

The second type of change is transitional. Transitional change is where the implications for the tangible change start to emerge. In the example, organisations operating Windows 10 could leverage some applications such as M.S. Teams, which impact work processes and how teams communicate, collaborate and work remotely. During the early stages of COVID-19, many organisations previously languishing over how to change working practices were suddenly thrown a lifeline by M.S. Teams as it offered the means to work remotely in a collaborative online space. That said, in countries moving out of lockdown, some organisations enforced a return to the office policy. Other organisations saw this as a transformational bridge to hybrid working. Remote working presented both challenges and opportunities for teams working remotely, but it was a stepping stone to a team's new identity.

Transformational

And that leads to the third type of change. Having the capability to work remotely and change working practices does make a transformation automatic. Transformation takes a different kind of approach to change: learning how to work differently, experimenting with what works and what doesn't, and, most importantly, a change in work habits and routines. Remote team working is increasingly the norm. Some organisations, like Spotify, have taken the step of transforming their business into fully remote. This fully remote model satisfies the third type of change transformational. Likely, this changing identity from an office-based organisation to a remote working organisation has changed the shape of the organisation. The underpinning system will change and morph to fit this new identity. In transformational change, there is a metamorphosis – the organisation has changed its shape and identity. In this new world, not only are self-organising teams possible, but they also underpin the basis of a shift to fully remote working.

The intangible nature of change

One of the reasons why change has moved to near number one priority for most organisations is the second part of the puzzle. It usually involves people, and that is the intangible aspect of change.

Working with teams on change is perhaps one of the most frustrating and yet rewarding aspects of coaching. The frustrating part is that most organisational change is still seen as a project or programme to be managed. While there are many good reasons to have a planning process and some critical elements for introducing change, the essential aspect of all change is that there will be a human-to-human interaction at some stage. And there's the rub. Even with information technology changes, as in the example moving to Windows 10, human beings are the recipients and users of the system. Customers may also be impacted by I.T. changes, mainly if you are introducing new features to inline applications. In his insightful paper on Wicked Problems (2008), Grint outlines a list of 10 issues that typically need addressing when introducing change. He adds that just following the list does not guarantee success. Each situation will be different because the context is different. The Wicked Problems he refers to occur because of complexity. In other words, when we add a tangible change into a human system, there may well be consequences beyond which we can plan.

1   An accepted need to change
2   A viable vision/alternative state
3   Change agents in place
4   Sponsorship from above
5   Realistic scale and pace change
6   An integrated transition programme
7   A symbolic end to the status quo
8   A plan for likely resistance
9   Constant advocacy
10 A locally owned benefits plan

Our role as coaches is to help the team counter some of the intangible aspects of change such as anxiety, uncertainty, insecurity and potential feelings of inadequacy – that we won't be able to bridge the gap.

During COVID-19 lockdowns, people turned to online video tools such as Zoom to run meetings and host workshops. In many cases, people were unfamiliar with the technology, and there was genuine anxiety about using the tool. In many online sessions in the early days of lockdown, time was spent teaching participants how to use the tool and reassuring them it was perfectly normal to feel overwhelmed with learning something new. In an interview on learner anxiety, Schein (2002) describes this internal process. He calls it learner anxiety because there is a paradox of the anxiety of unlearning something to learn something new.

If we accept Schein's argument, it is clear that the role of helping teams cope with change is to work with this paradox. A change to a process means learning a new work routine. We start to create stories such as 'I won't be able to do my work as efficiently, it will make slower'. Or we worry that we won't be able to perform our job as well and will be judged as underperforming by our bosses. We project out possible futures and start to fear the consequences of these changes both to how we perceive ourselves and to how others perceive us. This landscape is what we help teams navigate.

How do we help teams juggle this paradox? By decreasing anxiety of learning, we move the scales in favour of the change. The team coaching environment is a learning environment. Colart Miles calls the coach a 'learning accelerator'. Everything we do in setting up the team agreement, working together and role modelling **fearless learning** encourages the team to step into the learning zone.

How might you role model fearless learning as a coach? Here are some of the ways I model this in both team and group coaching.

Discovery phase

Ask questions about what they expect from their team coach and discuss how we can work together to reduce any learning anxiety. For example,

- What would help to create a great learning environment for this team?
- What currently gets in the way of creating a great learning environment?

Contracting/agreement phase

Discuss the learner anxiety equation – create a conversation and agree on how the team will model fearless learning for each other.

Explicitly contract around openness to experimentation. Describe what curiosity means. Agree on specific phrases team members will use. Start to teach protocols for introducing this into the sessions. For example, 'I'm curious to learn more about what you mean by . . . '

Contract around creating pauses.

Coaching phase

One team regularly ignored one specific member's input. During a session when most of the team were feverishly working around a flip chart, I noticed this one person side-lined from the conversation yet again. I was genuinely puzzled, so I called time out and asked the team for feedback on what they noticed about the group process. It was clear that amid busyness, they had missed the opportunity to bring everyone with them. As a learning experiment, it created the space to discuss how they worked together as a team. This situation was an example of using the pause button to aid the learning experience. In terms of team maturity, this team was on the starting line. The first stage was to help co-create processes the team could use to collaborate.

Another way I might role model fearless learning is by asking 'What's the question we need to address now?' or 'I'm not sure where we're heading – am I missing something?'

An experience I had a few years ago taught me the value and downsides of teaching phrases to team members to signify curiosity.

I was a participant in a workshop, and we split into smaller workgroups.

The discussion started, and we all shared something. One person bluntly interjected with 'Say more!'. It interrupted the flow of the conversation and delivered in such a blunt manner it felt more like an interrogation than curiosity. I felt taken back by the phrase and was puzzled by what happened. It was clear the person had learned this phrase and was practising with it – but it was incongruous and felt inauthentic.

Phrases by themselves are not necessarily going to work without an understanding of how you deliver them. Tonality and perhaps a softener, such as 'That's interesting, would you say more on that to help me understand?' would have encouraged the speaker.

In a team coaching environment, this would have been a great learning opportunity and pause for reflection.

National and organisational culture also plays a part in team behaviours because some national cultures are more direct. As a coach, we're constantly flexing our empathetic listening and sensitivity to learn and understand cultural markers to better work with the team.

When working with my co-author Gillian Jones-Williams' organisation, I learnt the acronym: T.E.D. – tell, explain, describe. It's a great reminder of how to model curiosity and lead the conversation in a way that encourages exploration and learning.

Tell:

- Tell me more about . . .
- Tell me about a time when you . . .

Explain

- I'm curious, can you explain a bit more?
- I'd like to understand. Can you explain a bit more?

Describe

- Maybe you can describe what that is like/happened, etc.
- What was going on for you in that situation?
- What might you be assuming about xyz?

Moving the status quo

We started this chapter by understanding the seemingly simple nature of change. Coaching self-organising teams is essentially a means of creating comfort with a moving status quo and equipped to embrace fearless learning. There will always be change in teams. Team members will come and go. The organisation may change its strategy, which will impact the purpose of the team. The leadership of the organisation may change. How the team copes with these natural ebbs and flows determines how well they perform. The added complexity with self-organising teams is that they're seeking to make sense of their own environment. Supportive sponsorship of the team and self-organising as a principle provides a base from which the team can develop and grow. The approach to managing change within the organisation is another challenge for teams.

Decomposing change into its parts is what happens in projects with a defined beginning, middle and end. The reality is usually far from this and, as Grint (2008) points out, likely to comprise clumsy solutions relying on finding practical wisdom that enables the organisation to move forward. His description of the leader as a Bricoleur, someone who can construct ideas and solutions using whatever comes to hand, is apposite for the team coaches and team members alike. Being comfortable with uncertainty and the ever-changing sands of the status quo enables teams to flow with change and allow the next piece of the puzzle to fit into place.

Pause for a moment and think about what this might mean for your coaching practice.

> How will you support teams in developing awareness of these challenges?
>
> What is your role in helping the team understand the organisational network?
>
> How will you work with the team and the sponsor(s) to support the creation of sufficient stability?
>
> What does sufficient stability look, feel and sound like for the team you are coaching?
>
> What capacity does the team have to cope with the change whilst staying on purpose?
>
> How will you and the team know when the team needs support?

One of the areas to cover in the discovery phase of the coaching assignment is around change. For example, how much change has the organisation experienced in the last 12–18 months? What change initiatives are in flight? What is the team's experience of that change? These questions help set the scene for the 'status-quo' – the version of 'normal' for this organisation. Each organisation will be different. One organisation had around 47 I.T. change projects in flight simultaneously – there were about 3,000 employees. The impact on the teams was significant – aside from resource challenges, the organisation was at capacity in terms of what it could digest. Understanding the organisation landscape before you start to work with the team is crucial if you are to help them cope and thrive on delivering value.

6.2   Locus of control and the importance of perceived choice

> Everything can be taken from a man but one thing: the last of the human freedoms – to choose one's attitude in any given set of circumstances. Viktor Frankl (2004)

The ability to flow with change comes from the team's sense of agency. How much control they believe that they have and their choices either elevate or reduce that sense of agency. Team coaching has a central tenet of teaching teams to coach themselves. One of the underlying principles aligned with **fearless learning** is **creating agency**. Let's explore the concept of locus of control.

Locus of control is a psychological term to describe how we perceive the degree of control we have over our lives versus external events. Locus simply means place – where do we place control. Is it within ourselves, or is it outside ourselves? A strong internal locus of control puts us in the centre of our universe and means we control the choices we make. Alternatively, if we believe that we are at the whims of others, our options will likely be restricted. Are we masters of our destiny or buffeted along with the tides of fortune? This question is one of the existential questions teams can face, especially when working in large corporate environments or organisations with a strong bureaucracy or institutionalised working habits.

A feeling that there is little control can lead teams to exhibit frustration and a sense of resignation on achieving tasks. In my research, I found much on the topic of learned helplessness. This term has been in use for many years. Helplessness describes the state of resignation when we try something multiple times and fail. We believe that further attempts are futile; therefore, we give up. The standard view of learned helplessness could explain why people fell back into an external locus of control frame. This view assumes that if events are beyond our control, what choice do we have but accept them? I have often experienced this working with teams, particularly going through organisational change. It can spread through a team. If one experiences a setback, others will fall in line with this mistaken belief that 'nothing can be done'.

In one of the most surprising finds during my research, I realised that learned helplessness is a default setting and not something that is learned – it is the baseline on which we as humans operate. Maier and Seligman (2016) reviewed learned helplessness and found that the research had got it the wrong way round. Helplessness, it turns out, is the default setting. We are designed to retreat when confronted with feedback. Our efforts are futile. In their paper, they explore the neuroscience behind why this is the case. The headline is helplessness is a programmed response to persistent and prolonged unpleasant events. Not only is it not learned, but it's also a default setting designed to protect.

Given this new perspective on why we stop trying, it's not surprising that teams give up when confronted with obstacles. At the end of their paper, they posit an interesting antidote to helplessness – hope. Hope blocks out the natural defence position of helplessness and provides a mechanism for moving forward. How might this knowledge help us coach teams? We can use these data to help teams explore and discuss:

1   It is natural to feel helpless, particularly when change is imminent or obstacles block the team from moving forward.
2   Creating a sense of control comes from a realisation that there is always hope for the future.

The role of the coach in this scenario is to provide extra information for the team to consider. The coach's role is to introduce a different perspective. All situations and obstacles are temporary. We can gain a sense of control by constraining the boundary and looking at the specific immediate impact for the team. This boundary creation leads to a great coaching conversation around 'What one thing can we do right now?' Today may not be the day to solve the global challenges, but we can start small and scale-up.

One of my favourite tools mentioned earlier uses Cartesian logic in Figure 6.2.

Teams often get stuck with decision making because they feel no sense of agency. Working through the four questions enables the team to free themselves from the tyranny of ever-decreasing circles and gain a new perspective that injects hope into the conversation.

Moving from left to right clockwise around the questions elicits moments of clarity and discussion. It also gets the team out of their way by challenging their thinking habits and is particularly helpful in moving from a default state of helplessness to hopefulness. The final two questions are designed as cognitive dissonance – stopping you in your tracks. Posting these questions up on the wall or using an online collaborative tool such as Jamboard means everyone can see

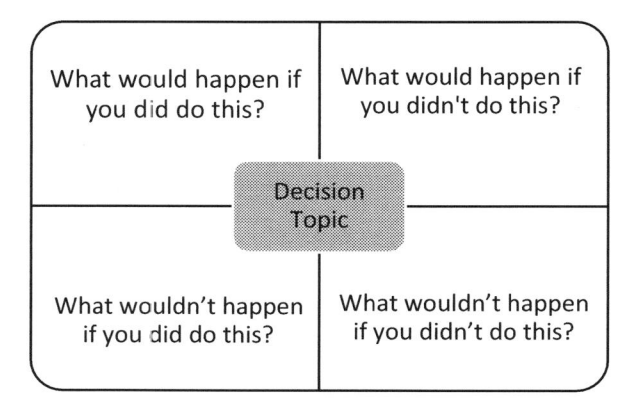

Figure 6.2 Cartesian Logic

their thinking. It helps get the team out of their head and look at their options from different perspectives.

In his book on learned hopefulness, Tomasulo (2020) comments that 'changing the brain's default position requires attention and effort'. The Cartesian logic activity enables the team to pay attention and requires effort to interrupt thinking patterns.

Another activity to help teams perceive a sense of control is to ask them to identify everything outside their control. What is getting in the way of them moving forward? We will call these constraints. These could be related to budgets, resources anything that the team feels they lack any control over. Using sticky notes or virtual sticky notes works well here because the team can colour code each constraint and place it on the wall or virtual wall for all to see.

Next, for each sticky note, the teams identify one small thing they could do today to reduce the impact of that constraint. Use a different colour sticky note and place it next to the constraint to which it relates. As the team moves through the constraints, ask them to identify possibilities for reducing the constraint. In doing this, the team will realise they do have control over certain things.

At the end of the activity, the team will have two lists of different coloured sticky notes. This visual representation of choice is essential in signalling to the team they do have agency even where they feel things are outside of their control. The following steps are for the team to decide what to do with the information. It could be that a prioritisation activity of the possibilities would be helpful. The team chooses what to do with the information.

A time for reflection is necessary so that the team can assess how they've travelled from their initial assumption that 'all is lost – we have no control' to a possible realisation that there are many things they could do. The key is the team has choices.

Our natural bias towards negative thinking influences our ability to see possibilities and hope. Increasing a sense of internal control enables the team to see a way forward. 'Hope involves agency to change things' Tomasulo (2020).

Coaching the team to shift perspective and create hopefulness as a default setting requires consistent and persistent challenge. If you as the coach observe the tam falling into a downward spiral, asking 'what could you do about this?' acts as a trigger on the team to be hopeful. Coaching teams is a process of transference: transferring the practice of asking questions and providing space for election and possible. We are teaching the team how to develop an internal locus of control. Ultimately, the team will transition to self-coaching. Our role is to facilitate learning of coaching skills, techniques and approaches to ignite a readiness to embrace possibility. We also help the team walk the tightrope of parados – that external controls also serve a purpose. Teams exist within a wider ecosystem and complexity. As we've discussed, there will be related but not necessarily known consequences with every action. Agency with responsibility is the mission for coaching teams. Helping embrace possibility also requires discernment.

Let's circle back to Viktor Frankl. The key message of his book, *Man's Search for Meaning*, is choice – that we can always choose our path regardless of our life situation. Helping teams develop possibilities teaches them they always have a choice. Each choice has a consequence – either known or unknown. Coaching self-organising teams entails working together to co-create **deliberate practices** around decision making and coping with change. The anchor for these choices is the team's purpose. Creating agency starts with a shared purpose. Everything the team does and learns stems from that purpose. The only certain thing is change. Teams that thrive in complexity and uncertainty can retain a sense of control by realising that they have agency to choose what they do. Sometimes those choices might be limited. Sometimes they might not – a team that can flex as the situation demands means they can adapt and see change as a necessary result of growth.

> 'Some things are in our control and others not. Things in our control are opinion, pursuit, desire, aversion, and, in a word, whatever are our own actions. Things not in our control are body, property, reputation, command, and, in one word, whatever are not our own actions'. Epictetus.

6.3 The two mindsets – fixed and growth

The sub-heading for this final piece of the puzzle could be resilience. Professor Carol Dweck's groundbreaking research in education has permeated the business world and led to many changes in the way we view learning both at school and at work. Her research centred on the power of beliefs – that they can determine your success. A fundamental tenet of her research is that it is possible to grow your talents and Intelligence Quotient. Her book (2008) describes the implications of this – that we can all learn how to reach our potential. She names two mindsets: fixed and growth. Dweck is now one of the most well-known psychologists through her work on the growth mindset (Dweck 2008) and her T.E.D. talk of 2014.

Here's a simple definition of the two mindsets: a fixed mindset sees intelligence and talent as an innate ability – you're either smart and talented or not. A growth mindset sees an opportunity for development through deliberate practice. A characteristic of a growth mindset is the willingness to pursue a learning goal even though it might be challenging and create discomfort. Those children who were willing to learn by doing, making mistakes and having another go demonstrated increased abilities and increased their I.Q. The key to fostering a growth mindset is creating an environment in which it can flourish. Helping co-create an environment where experimentation and learning are routine and where everyone is encouraged to stay the course even when there are setbacks is the team coach's domain.

Her research has come under scrutiny in recent years, and an interview with Professor Robert Plomin (Lee and Wiggins 2015), a behavioural genetics professor, argues that persistence is influenced by genetics. This genetic link suggests that not everyone will have the ability to persist, therefore, grow as per the growth mindset. Shenk (2011) provides a counter-argument to the genetics debate arguing that epigenetics plays an integral part in developing talent. And Dweck herself, in an interview with Tes Podagogy podcast, contends that the nuances of the research have been missed (2017).

What does this all mean for coaching teams? First, it's essential to recognise Dweck herself states the mindsets are not binary – we are a mixture of both. There will be certain situations where we exhibit positive learning motivation and others where we want to give up. It's tempting to coach teams to do their best and keep going. Exhortation alone will not help. Let's return to contracting – agreeing on how we'll work with the team. When we co-create how we'll work together, we're setting the scene for a growth mindset. Ask questions that elicit the opportunity for learning to take place. For example, what sort of environment will we create to support experimentation and acknowledge that not everything will work or work the first time?

It's essential to recognise the context the team is working in too. How well does the organisation handle learning from its mistakes? What are the consequences the team has experienced of perceived mistakes or failures? How will the team handle perceived failure? How do they cope with paradox? Creating space for thinking and reflecting is a critical aspect of developing a growth mindset. Helping teams figure out what's happening and working together to form a way forward. These first steps help foster a growth mindset. When linked with a strong sense of agency to change things and fearless learning, the team can explore its actual capability.

- Creating a safe environment for experimentation
- Discussing the necessary role of failure in the learning process
- Handling paradox
- Creating space for thinking and reflecting
- Experimentation is an essential part of learning
- Acknowledge the broader context

The attainment of a growth mindset can be very seductive. Here's where I offer a different perspective and refer to Gorell (2013), where I discuss the notion of talent as a fixed commodity. Growth is a continual state of change. The very word means the process of growing. Coaching teams to self-organise is a process of development. In some conversations, the labels fixed and growth mindset can become weaponised and a source of conflict. When we understand that there is a continuum, we move between it creates an opportunity for conversation. What are the bounds the team operates within? Returning to Plomin (Lee and Wiggins 2015), there may well be times that the team doesn't have the capacity or capability to do something, and they need to seek help elsewhere. In our eagerness to coach the team, we sometimes miss the signals that the team is at a point where they really can't just 'push through' it. That's a signal to take stock and reflect on the reality of the situation. Jason Little sums up this moment of realisation nicely:

> I think nowadays one of the things is, just never having worked on a software team. So it's hard to understand what a software team is going through. If you've never had to deliver something and detaching from the reality of some organizations. Like, one of the telecoms I worked for, school and Christmas was always the biggest seasons for them. So, you talk about very hard deadlines, usually fixed scope, fixed time, which never works. And big code freezes like the whole month of December. Everything's locked down. And I think coaches that haven't lived through stuff like that will look at the agile coaching playbook. 'Oh, well, you should be doing continuous delivery. You shouldn't be freezing your code for a month'. And so they, they don't understand the context of the enterprise business.

In this situation, it would be easy to think the team was operating with a fixed mindset – but the context was the determinant of the team's actions.

The growth mindset in relation to change is a way of thinking about growing the team's capacity to learn together as a whole system. Clutterbuck (2020) talks about building a learning team and the fact that it is an 'evolutionary process'. A growth mindset is just that – growing a team set up to learn as the coaching conversations evolve. If we return to the definition of change outlined at the beginning of this chapter – a move from the status quo – it's apparent that there will be inherent learning in the move from the status quo. Without learning, the status quo remains. The coaching process is a **deliberate practice** for learning together as a system – in essence, and it is the means to develop a growth mindset. Helping teams self-organise in a way that embraces learning means the organisation creates both capacities for change and learning through the team coaching process.

6.4   Chapter summary

Change is a pervasive theme and part of reality both at work and at home. Most teams will have to work through change at some point, and the ability to not only survive but thrive will make the difference.

- Helping teams cope with change is an increasingly important aspect of our coaching work.
- Change means many things to many people. Essentially change is a move from the status quo.
- There are three types of change: transactional, transitional and transformational. Knowing where you're starting from and understanding the direction of travel help create actions.
- We cannot be sure of the consequences of changes we make. There is no obvious cause and effect in a complex system, and there may well be unintended consequences. Teams can become adept at working in a complex system when they are given support.
- Fearless learning is a means of coping with change and offsets a natural tendency to learner anxiety. Coaches act as learning accelerators.
- Create a sense of agency within the team so, no matter what, they operate from a position of choice.
- Learned helplessness is a default setting. Or rather, helplessness is a default. It's not something we learn. It takes effort, therefore, to move away from helplessness into hopefulness.
- Cartesian logic helps the brain create choice by challenging thinking patterns and getting us to step out of unconscious choice into conscious choice.
- The two mindsets – fixed and growth – are not binary. We are a mixture of both. Self-organisation is a process of development. The coach and team must give thought and consideration if they want to adopt a growth mindset.
- The coaching process is a deliberate practice for learning together as a team.

Bibliography

Clutterbuck, D. (2020) *Coaching The Team At Work – The Definitive Guide to Team Coaching*. London, UK: Nicholas Brealey Publishing.

Dweck, C. S. (2008) *Mindset: The New Psychology of Success*. New York, NY: Ballantine Books Trade Paperback Edition.

Dweck, C. S. (2017) Professor Carol Dweck on Growth Mindset Theory and Her Critics. *TES Pedadgogy Podcast*. https://www.tes.com/news/professor-carol-dweck-growth-mindset-theory-and-her-critics. Accessed April 7, 2021.

Frankl, V. (2004) *Man's Search For Meaning*. London: Rider Books.

George Long (translator). (2005) *Enchiridion and Selections from the Discourses of Epictetus*. Digireads.com (January 1, 2005).

Gorell, R. (2013) *Group Coaching; A Practical Guide to Optimizing Collective Talent in Any Organization*. London: Kogan Page.

Grint, K. (2008) Wicked Problems and Clumsy Solutions: The Role of Leadership. In: Brookes, S., and Grint, K. (eds.), *The New Public Leadership Challenge*, vol. 1, pp. 169–186. Basingstoke: Palgrave Macmillan.

The Growth Mindset Institute. www.growthmindsetinstitute.org/growth-mindset/growth-mindset-resources/.

Lee, J., and Wiggins, K. (2015) *Growth Mindset Theory Is 'Overplayed' and Could Be Harmful, Geneticist Warns*. TES online. www.tes.com/news/growth-mindset-theory-overplayed-and-could-be-harmful-geneticist-warns. Accessed April 10, 2021.

Lundström, A., and Westerdahl, A. (2021) *Introducing Working from Anywhere*. HR Blog Spotify. https://hrblog.spotify.com/2021/02/12/introducing-working-from-anywhere/. Accessed March 27, 2021.

Maier, S. F., and Seligman, M. E. P. (2016) Learned Helplessness at Fifty: Insights from Neuroscience. *Psychological Review*, vol. 123, no. 4, pp. 349–367. https://doi.org/10.1037/rev0000033.

Schein, E. (2002) *The Anxiety of Learning – The Darker Side of Organizational Learning Diane L*. Coutu Harvard Business School. https://hbswk.hbs.edu/archive/edgar-schein-the-anxiety-of-learning-the-darker-side-of-organizational-learning. Accessed June 11, 2021.

Shenk, D. (2011) *The Genius in All of Us: Why Everything You've Been Told about Genetics, Talent and Intelligence Is Wrong*. London: Icom Books.

Tomasulo, D. (2020) *Learned Hopefulness the Power of Positivity to Overcome Depression*. Oakland, Canada: New Harbinger Publications, Inc.

Chapter 7

Knowing when to quit

Our prime directive as team coaches is to leave the team capable of coaching itself. Our role is to reduce reliance on us as the coach and rely on each other instead. We should be explicit upfront about how long we think the team needs coaching. Being clear on coaching duration applies to internal team coaches, Agile coaches or external coaches. It is easier for external coaches to discuss this as there is an expectation the coaching will not be a permanent assignment. It is often not as explicit for internal coaches and Agile coaches and usually revolves around a particular project. The Agile Coach's prime directive, even in these situations, is to equip the team with sufficient capability to coach itself, even if this means that the coach only engages with them for a small portion of the project life cycle.

The discovery process supports this part of the scoping phase, as the discoveries we make before we start working with the team will indicate the coaching assignment's likely duration. Things we learn in discovery form part of the contracting or agreement phase and help give direction to the purpose of the coaching process and indicate to both the team and other stakeholders the goal of self-management. Moreover, if we do not specifically contract at the start how long the coaching will last, we can run into the challenge of the team relying on us instead of their ability to self-manage.

We often develop deep relationships with the people we coach. The coaching space encourages sharing and leads to realisations and what we call 'Aha' moments. Over investment in our coachees can tempt us to continue coaching the team beyond what they need. As coaches, we need to be vigilant about this and seek support from the process we use to engage with stakeholders. In short, if we as coaches have a framework and process with some fundamental principles agreed to upfront, we will be better positioned to exit stage left when the team is ready.

This chapter covers the vital phase of transitioning or transferring the team to self-coaching as an autonomous unit. During the coaching sessions, the coach or coaches will be gradually reducing the team's reliance on them to coach. To explore this further, here's one of the ways my business partner and I do this. We use a Hot Seat Coaching tool based on Reg Revan's Action Learning Sets described briefly previously.

We start by taking the team through the process. This process includes coaching the team as we go through each stage and culminates in a debrief session where

DOI: 10.4324/9781003110583-8

we discuss the coaching content – exploring insights, learning, surprises and so on, followed by a debrief on the coaching process itself. For the next round, we invite someone else into the hot seat and ask one of the team members to coach the team through the process. Afterwards, we conduct a learning review to discover how they found it and how the group experienced the coaching. This process is an efficient way of helping the team learn a coaching process that is simple to understand and implement. It does require careful setting up to ensure that there is sufficient safety to sit in the 'hot seat' and the 'ground rules' are clear before they start.

We find that teams quickly learn how to conduct a 'hot seat' coaching session and gain confidence to continue the process on their own the next time. Over time the team can bring in more sophisticated questioning, challenging both their assumptions and those of the person in the 'hot seat'. This transfer of skills and knowledge on a simple coaching process prepares the team in three ways:

1 Teaching – the process is something that can be learned and applied immediately
2 Coaching – the coaches demonstrate how to coach on both content and process through questioning, listening, reflection and curiosity
3 Role modelling – curiosity as coaches – providing a frame of reference to experiment and explore what works and doesn't work with the team

Once the team learns the process, it provides a basis for building other coaching skills at subsequent sessions where the team can leverage the coach's skills to enhance, adjust and develop the basic premise.

Hot seat coaching is just one example of how we are continually preparing the team for handover during the coaching assignment. Each session provides an opportunity to learn about coaching by being coached. Review or retrospectives form a vital role in the lifecycle of team coaching and are a great way of making tacit learning overt. The retrospective will be our starting point as we go on a voyage of discovery through the many alleyways of capturing the learning.

7.1 Retrospective and pre-mortems

For the team

In one-on-one coaching, it is usual to spend some time at the end of each session reviewing how the session went.

> What did the individual learn? What actions are they going to take? What went well in the session? What surprised them? What was the best thing to come out of the session? Where did they find it most challenging? How did the session land versus what they were expecting?

Team coaching follows a similar process. This process of reflecting on the immediate experience captures the learning whilst it is fresh in the mind of the team members and enables iteration and improvement for the next session. The team captures the learning and identifies one or two things on which to take action. These moments of reflection have become known as retrospectives because they look back on what has happened.

The practice of ending each session with reflection starts the habit of continuous improvement. The team can use the collected retrospectives to conclude the coaching assignment as a resource to reflect on the overall journey. One question I use to prompt learning at this global level is, 'How has this coaching experience increased your capability as a team?'

The process

I give each team member a few minutes to write down their thoughts on sticky notes. These can be either virtual or physical sticky notes using an application like Google Jamboard. When everyone has captured their individual ideas, the team allocates an amount of time for the conversation. For example, 30 minutes with ten reflection thoughts equals three minutes of discussion per thought. Taking each sticky note in turn, set the timer for three minutes. The team member who wrote that particular reflection thought describes their thoughts. For any time left, they invite others to contribute to the conversation. At the end of the three minutes, the next team member shares their reflection point. Go round the room, calling on each team member one at a time. If a team member has made more than one reflection thought, do another round. The idea is that everyone has an opportunity to speak for at least three minutes, in this example, before the next person shares their learning. In a virtual environment, it's helpful to record and transcribe these conversations. In a face-to-face environment, you could jot down notes on a flip chart for the team. It might be helpful for the team to review the reflections for any themes that have emerged. The conversation would naturally move on to 'What else could we do as a team to build on what we've achieved together?' You can follow the same process allowing everyone to write down their thoughts first and then work out how long you have for the total conversation and translate this into time allocation per idea. This approach to retrospectives in a team coaching environment combines both facilitation skills and coaching skills – facilitation in terms of a process by which the team members can hold that retrospective conversation (the outcome) coaching to ask questions that get the team to contribute together.

The previous example is only one way of running a retrospective, and a Google search will return hundreds of different ways of doing retrospectives. The team decides what format will work best for them and allows them to experiment with a different kind of retrospective at the end of each session. Over time, the team will learn the best way to review learning for them as a team. The team learns for itself, and your role is to provide an opportunity for them to explore using the resources and tools you have and inviting them to come up with their own. Here's an example of a session framework.

During the contracting phase of the coaching agreement – invite the team to take responsibility for the end review at each session. Explain the overarching framework for each session:

- At the beginning of each session, we will agree on an outcome for the session
- We will recap our team agreement on how we're going to work together in the session
- We will work on the topic at hand during the session
- At the end of each session, we will do a post-session retrospective

Invite each team member to come up with a way of doing a post-session retrospective for the end of each session. Agree at the first session that a team member will coach/lead each of the session retrospectives. For example, the coach guides the first session retrospective to demonstrate what this means. At the end of the first session, ask for a volunteer to lead the next session retrospective.

Agreeing on who will take on the coaching role for the retrospective before the session means that they have time to prepare and deliver the retrospective approach. At the penultimate session, agree on how the team will review the whole coaching assignment and how much you will actively coach in the session and how much the team will coach. Slowly but surely, you are exiting stage left from the coaching process. You are setting up an expectation that this will be the case from the beginning of the coaching relationship. Beginning with the end in mind, as the saying goes, means that the team is not surprised when you ask them to become more actively involved in coaching each other and learning for themselves. Your presence in the room is to help create space for the team to step into and explore their learning and the coaching process itself.

For the coach

Often as coaches, we want to feel that we must do something active to coach. Yet, we perhaps forget that our presence in the room will change the dynamic in the coaching session. Even though we might not be doing or saying anything in the session, our presence impacts the team. We can take that opportunity to step out of the process and enable the team to step into the process.

By being present but not active in the session, we create a space that invites others into the conversation. The team can always ask for help if they want it during the process, and again this is something you might want to agree with the team. 'How much input do you need from me/us as we evolve together?' At the beginning of each session, you re-contract around that intervention. 'Today, how are you feeling? What do you want from me/us in how I/we coach the session?' Again, if you're co-coaching the team, you both need to feel comfortable that you will be taking less and less of an active role in the coaching sessions.

We can sometimes feel we want to step in and rescue the team, particularly if we know from our experience the team is likely going down a bit of an alleyway. It's very tempting to step in. Part of our learning process is that the team has to have those experiences to learn for itself. After they've had that experience, asking the team, 'Would it be useful to review what happened there?' presents the team with an opportunity for further learning. They may or may not take up the offer. Again, there might be a reason for that, or it might be they just want to move on. Knowing when to let go is part of our learning as coaches. Edgar Schein (1999) talks about the importance of timing. When the team is ready to revisit this, they will – it might be that today is not the time to do that. Context is everything, and sometimes teams need an opportunity to go off track. Something might have happened in the organisation that you are not privy to. It might have just happened before they came into the physical or virtual room. We always exercise judgement when we coach – which questions to ask, which approaches to take and when to let go. These are moments for us to learn and, where possible, share those learnings with the team too. We are both part and separate from the system in which they work. That system is in constant flow and leads to the next opportunity for retrospection.

In Jones and Gorell (2021), we outline some questions for the coach to use for self-reflection after each coaching session. I have adapted these to work in a team coaching environment at Table 7.1.

The questions are designed as a starting point. You could integrate some of the retrospective questions such as what you liked about the session, what you learned during the session and what you would change next time in how you coach the session. If you are working with a co-coach, you could answer the questions individually and share your answers. These questions are an excellent prompt for a conversation about how you are developing your practice together. Reflection on your own coaching practise draws out your learning and helps identify potential themes about how the team is working that you might not be conscious of in the flow of coaching. The specific questions you ask will change as your practice develops. In the early days of coaching teams, the emphasis will likely be on coaching skills. Over time the questions will become more about the broader systems and context of the coaching. Creating a habit of reflection and retrospection, documenting what you learn, is a means of tracking progress. You can use this to produce a development plan for your team coaching skills and how you co-coach with others.

Table 7.1 Team Coach Self-Reflection

How well did you:

Prepare for the coaching session?

Help the team set an outcome for the session?

Help the team identify areas where they might revert to previous behaviours?

Help the team develop strategies for maintaining progress?

Provide sufficient support and challenge?

Serve as a role model?

Encourage the team to generate a wide range of alternative approaches or solutions, which they could consider together?

Observe non-verbal behaviour carefully and check for incongruence?

Separate observations from judgements?

Use skilful and powerful questioning to promote sharing of insights and learning?

Create the space for the team to give feedback to each other?

Share your observations and feedback?

Help the team?

Reflections

What were some of the key moments of insight for you about how your coaching is helping the team?

What questions led to moments of insight for the team?

What was most challenging about today's session?

What was the reason for that?

What were the key standout moments for the team during the session?

How did you contribute to supporting autonomy within the team during the session?

How well did you work with your co-coach (if you have one)?

How might you improve how you work together with your co-coach (if you have one)?

What have you observed in the coaching that might be about the wider system?

How might this be present during the sessions?

What other questions would it be useful to reflect on?

What are the key opportunities for further development?

Key actions:

What happens when team members change?

Teams are dynamic, and it's unlikely that team members will be the same during the coaching assignment. Even with permanent teams, people resign and leave organisations. Stakeholders change too, which impacts the team. If it's a key stakeholder or sponsor of the team, this can have a significant impact. Sometimes, destabilising the team's purpose, in a worst-case scenario, leads to disbanding of the team.

The ability to learn and pre-flect – that is, think about what might happen – helps create resilience and the ability to flex. We can use retrospectives to signify the end of a phase in the lifecycle of the team. When members leave the team, it is a great time to pause and reflect. A simple retrospective can be helpful. One way of doing this is using three headings: liked, learned and let go. Using these three headings provides an opportunity for team members to share what they might need to let go of now that a particular team member is leaving. And for the team member who is leaving, it provides an opportunity to transition gracefully from the team. An activity I ran with one team that proved very powerful was a sticky note gratitude ceremony.

> Give each person a pad of sticky notes. They write one thing they are grateful for about each team member on a sticky note. When everyone has finished writing their gratitude notes, they hand out the notes to each team member – first, saying 'Thank You' and then explaining what they're grateful for about that particular team member. The recipient team member merely says 'Thank you' in return. They go around each team member until they have given out all of the sticky notes.

In this activity, everyone must have a sticky note from each of the other team members. This process focuses the team on showing gratitude for everyone in the team. In the previous chapter on change, we talked about the importance of gratitude. This gratitude activity is potent. I have seen teams who reluctantly take part at first and then realise how it changes their attitude to their teammates by focusing on what they're grateful for instead of focusing on problems. It's a wonderful way for team members to leave the team too. And for teams where there is a powerful bond helps them cope with the team member's loss.

The simple liked, learned, letting go and sticky note gratitude activity combined provides a powerful way of creating an ending for the team to step into a new beginning. Inviting new team members into space offers an opportunity for pre-flection and pre-mortems. Let's explore how these can help the team move into the next phase of maturity.

Pre-flection and pre-mortems

Let us revisit the concept of pre-mortems from an earlier chapter. We're reviewing it here to understand how this might help the team adapt when new members join. There's another concept I'd like to introduce, which is related but not the same, and that's pre-flection. This word encapsulates the thinking required yet often neglected when team members change. We assume that the 'team' is still the same, and yet it has transformed into something different. The dynamic will be different. Existing team members will probably feel allegiances to each other, and a new member joining goes through a process of learning how to work within the team and become part of the team. Similarly, the team has to learn how to embrace and welcome the new team member.

Edmondson and Harvey (2017) explore some of the different models of team maturity and characterise it as sequential as per Tuckman (1965) and Bennis and Shepard (1956) or non-sequential as per Gersick (1988) and McGrath (1991). In Gersick's research, two interesting factors relating to how teams form and reform emerge. The first is the importance of the first meeting. The first meeting sets the tone for the remaining lifespan of the team. When a new member joins the team, it is as if the team is forming for the first time and becomes the 'first' meeting for the new team. It is an excellent opportunity to share the learning from the previous work with the new team member and take a pause to think about what next. Here's a different way of using pre-mortems described in an earlier chapter.

Invite the team to think about two scenarios.

- Ask one half of the team to imagine the team in six months – think about all the things that could possibly have gone wrong in terms of processes, interactions, task completion and so on. For ease, think of these as potholes.
- Ask the other half of the team to imagine the team in six months – think about all the things that could possibly have gone well in terms of processes, interactions, task completion and so on. For ease, think of these as energisers.
- Suggested timing is 20 minutes – after which ask the teams to share their thoughts.
- Using both halves' input – invite them to develop ways to introduce the energisers and reduce the likelihood of falling in the potholes.

The use of pre-mortems encourages the team to discuss some of the obstacles that might occur to produce action instead of as a downward spiral discussion. The introduction of a new member presents the opportunity to pause and reflect on the team's progress, take stock and voice some of their concerns creatively. The latest member's input is valuable because it is given without prior knowledge of how the team has worked to date.

Pre-flection is a similar approach to pre-mortems and another way of introducing new members and reforming the team. It is a word that emerged from my thinking about how teams form and reform. A Google search resulted in a short but illustrative article, Falk (1995), that beautifully explains the process of preflection – a simple process of inviting comments on how the team participants will feel after an experience. Its simplicity and documenting of feelings before something happens make it a great tool to use as the retrospective process. For example, capture comments when the team reforms, a new member joins or an existing member leaves. 'How will we feel about our team experience in the future?' Every three months, the team can revisit their statements and discuss the experience. A simple retrospective could include any or all of the following questions:

- What did we get right?
- What surprised us?
- What do we want more of?
- What else might we feel in the future?

The second factor in Gersick's (1988) research is the importance of mid-term reviews. Her research focuses on project teams that naturally have a beginning and endpoint. The clarity of start and end makes the mid-point a temporally easy place to spot. Coaching stable teams, i.e. where there is no project per se on which the team is working, means that a mid-term review becomes a regular review. The team decides how often they wish to do this, and the suggestion would be every two to three months to see how they're tracking. Teams often get stuck in the busyness of task completion and perhaps don't spend enough time reviewing progress in longer-term continuous work. In the context of team self-organisation, this would include both the process and interrelational aspects of the team and the tangible outcomes the team has produced. Gersick (1988) also provides insight on the importance of context. We have explored the complex nature of teams within organisations – their maturation and development. Teams do not develop in a vacuum, and the organisational context in which they build influence all aspects of the team. The wider system is ever-present in how the team works together and the nature of the interpersonal relationships. The process is one aspect of team development – but it's not the only thing the team should be reviewing. Building a review timetable helps the team take regular pauses in how they're doing. It also provides an opportunity to refresh the team's perspective on purpose and change things up, so the team develops rather than stagnates.

Retrospectives, pre-mortems and pre-flection are resources the team can use to denote endings and beginnings. They're a means of helping the team transition to the next phase in their development. They also provide a neat way of transferring the coaching mantle to the team and transitioning to fully self-organising. Many organisations moving towards a self-organising model engage coaches and have internal coaches working within the organisation to help teams master self-organisation. How this happens and which organisations seem to prosper from this approach is the next step in our story.

7.2 Self-organising gone viral

Buurtzorg is one of the companies most often cited as an exemplar of a self-perpetuating, self-organising system. Having set up the company in 2006 spurred on by frustrations in the home care sector, Jos De Blok has seen the organisation grow from a handful of people to around 15,000 nursing staff, 50 back-office staff, 21 coaches and two directors. Having worked my way through articles, YouTube clips and blog posts, it's clear why this organisation is the vanguard of self-organising teams. I have referenced some of my research resources in the notes. The focus, though, is on the coaching of these teams.

Teams in Buurtzorg are purposely kept small and have to fit around an IKEA table – one of the heuristics De Blok outlines that explains his simple and easy to understand approach. Each team, therefore, has a maximum of 12 people who each have responsibility for up to five patients. The goal of this setup is to ensure that the patient receives continuity and quality of care. There is also a strong focus on highly qualified nurses, with over 65% of all nurses holding a bachelor's degree – see Centre for Public Impact blog (2018). Nursing is the primary role for each person within the team; additionally, there are non-nursing roles; Nandram (2015) mentions the team needs to fulfil to ensure that the team is fully functional. This includes

- Housekeeper
- Planner
- Informer
- Developer
- Mentor

In this sense, the team is self-organising and an autonomous unit able to call on the centre for support when needed. The regional coaches are few, and their role is to help when the teams get stuck with problems they can't resolve and best practice input.

Each team is trained in a type of solutions-focused coaching developed by Ben Wenting and Astrid Vermeer of The Institute for Cooperative issues. The team members are also taught a form of peer coaching called Intervisie – see Kaloudis blog (2016). This approach to peer coaching looks pretty similar to hot seat coaching mentioned elsewhere in this book. The combination of the two coaching methods provides a great foundation to help the team:

- Run effective meetings – there is a chair's framework to help with facilitating the meeting
- Share a standard protocol for having challenging conversations. The protocol provides a safe framework for dialogue. There is a keen focus on language: 'what do you propose?' 'Do you have any other suggestions?' (see Ben Wenting's (2013) YouTube clips with staged meetings to demonstrate how this works in practice.)
- Clear definition of what consensus means – reaching an agreement is through debate
- Peer-to-peer coaching based on helping each other – similar to hot seat coaching

A solution-focused approach is vital, so the teams spend as little time analysing the problem. It is easy to understand why this is important for Buurtzorg foundered against a context of overly analysed and compartmentalised health problems which drove efficiency at the cost of both effectiveness and patient health. The neighbourhoods in which the teams work and how the team members do their jobs are inextricably linked. There is a strong sense of helping patients live independent lives.

The regional coaches act as best practice conduits and a support resource for navigating problems the teams cannot resolve. The team is responsible for hiring and firing members, should it come to that, and having an external resource on which they can call. Technology plays a big part in how the team works and collaborates with other teams, both from knowledge sharing and managing their teams. In RACI terms, the roles are clear and the responsibilities are outlined in detail. The team set up is designed for success – they receive relevant training and can request other training as the need arises. They form and start their neighbourhood network, recruiting patients through their community contacts. The size constraints on teams, i.e. no more than 12 members with five patients per team member, ensure that the teams know the scope. They create an autonomous unit operating within a specific neighbourhood with clear guidelines on achievements – 60% billable hours.

The role of coaching within the teams focuses on self-management from inception. Teaching the team protocols, giving them tools and techniques that to put into immediate practice echo the ethos of the organisation – help patients self-manage and lead independent lives. In this sense, Buurtzorg is an example of creating a coaching culture and ensuring that it develops a life of its own.

- Create simple protocols so that teams can learn to coach and manage themselves
- Create a shared language, e.g. 'what do you propose?'
- Define roles clearly – e.g. the meeting chair/facilitator role
- Identify the scope of the team responsibilities
- Develop the teams around autonomy and self-management from the start – treat each team like a startup environment
- Consensus – based on joint responsibility
- Ownership – the team owns both its success and shortcomings
- Clarity of expectations on what 'good' performance looks like
- Make the team task interdependent – help the team create self-sufficiency
- Encourage innovation – expectations of the teams know are transparent so that they know what to achieve so allow the teams to come up with different and new ways of doing this – free from corporate mandates
- Create a team system that maps onto the organisation's mission – empowered patients in the case of Buurtzorg

Coaching in Buurtzorg is integrated with how the team operates daily. It's not something that's done to the team, but the team does something for itself. The self-organising team approach mirrors their hope for their patients – self-managed and independent living.

Buurtzorg has achieved the holy grail of coaching gone viral – an authentic coaching culture. The company has inspired many other organisations to experiment with self-organising teams. I spoke with different people throughout researching this book, and a recurring theme of experimentation, trial and error was a shared experience. There was also a vital element of approaching work differently: to turn the old model of leader and subordinates on its head. I was excited and curious to learn of one organisation here in Perth, Western Australia, one of the most isolated cities in the world and thousands of kilometres away from the Netherlands, had taken up the challenge of seeing how self-organising teams might work. Ian Jackson, Director of People and Culture in an academic institution, intrigued by an HBR article by Hamel (2011), started a book club to introduce the concept of self-organisation through Kirkpatrick's book *Beyond Empowerment* (2017). The sharing in the book club led to a broader interest in the idea within his organisation and made him wonder how he could 'strike the first match'.

> So I decided that I would pilot it in a span of control that I was able to, which was with our HR business partners. And I thought, . . . if we're going to grow the island, the HR business partner is going to be key.

He created a bubble for the self-organising team to operate and used the holacracy approach, which has a clear framework of how self-organising teams work. He appointed one person as the key resource investigator. Their role was to explore the concept, talk with people who were already using the model and bring it back to the organisation. The organisation knew that there was a team of six people experimenting with self-organisation. The challenge was the two systems operating at the same time. The team worked well in relation to organising itself, and the challenge was the interface with the rest of the organisation.

What was interesting about Jackson's experiment was the preparation for the team working together. They followed Kirkpatrick's model (2017) and created rules of engagement that Jackson reflects are not dissimilar to things you might find in an Enterprise Agreement (an agreement between employers and employees for collective bargaining). One of Kirkpatrick's questions asks the team to address how you might dismiss a team member who isn't performing. Straight off the blocks, the process asks the team to consider some of the thorny issues within organisations. Addressing thorny issues at the beginning of a team's development naturally requires a strong agreement within the team and, crucially, setting up psychological safety from the get-go and having a formal model for self-organisation such as the holacracy model helps.

The experiment ran for 12 months. During this time, Jackson noticed that the team started to exhibit changes in how they managed performance and interacted with each other and the organisation.

> [T]he level of collaboration and communication between them picked up enormously. They just previously thought they didn't need each other. They weren't really a team. . . . Secondly, the performance expectation, you know, going through the holacracy expectation of what you commit to or, in Doug's (Kirkpatrick) language doing what you say you're going to do, and have transparency and kindness for each other. All of a sudden, performance management was happening amongst colleagues. . . . To see the level of engagement around that at a peer and colleague level, I found fascinating.

The team, in this case, sought help outside the organisation in the form of someone who had direct experience of working in a holacratic organisation – Doug Kirkpatrick. Rather than coaching the team, he provided mentoring and training in the process and methods by which the team could work autonomously. One team member provided the learning direction for the team and acted as the resource investigator, or to use Jackson's terminology, the accelerator of knowledge because they'd done the deep dive on the process. They were not the leader, but they had a deep level of knowledge to help them adopt the holacratic principles. The experiment was interrupted by COVID-19, and in Jackson's words, the Mothership had to take over. The team members all benefitted from the experience and developed a greater sense of agency in the organisation's changes. Knowing when to let go is as essential for the coach as it is for the organisation. In the following section, we'll explore some key themes and continue developing quasi guidelines for knowing when to quit.

7.3 Letting go – knowing when to move on

If our prime directive as coaches is to leave the team capable of coaching itself, we should consider our directive concerning the organisation. Naturally, our focus is to work with the team and understand how we can help the team develop capability. In complex adaptive systems, we are always vicariously coaching the organisation when we coach the team. During the discovery phase, we will have spoken with key stakeholders to gain a contextual understanding of the team. Additionally, we will glean essential clues about how the team might develop their organisation and how their development might impact the organisation. It always surprises me to hear organisations that decide to adopt Agile or go for Agile at scale wondering why teams are sub optimised. Self-organising might be one of the Agile principles, but this does require a deeper review of the organisational system in which the teams will be supported, or not, in their quest. In the same way, organisations wishing to coach teams to become more self-organising cannot put the genie back in the bottle when they realise autonomy might challenge the organisational status quo.

One organisation, Buffer, decided to adopt self-organisation wholesale and realised that something wasn't quite right after a year of experimenting with the approach, Widrich (August 2015). Their approach was to remove all hierarchy and give individuals complete freedom to choose what they worked on. They took away some supporting structures such as one-to-one meetings and guidelines on what to work on. It seems that there was a proliferation of lots of projects with very little focus and a somewhat chaotic approach to the work they were doing. The experiment detrimentally affected both employee and customer experience – the exact opposite of what they hoped. They realised that to become self-organising, you have to have structure.

The Goldilocks principle on structure

We learned from the Buurtzorg example that self-organising teams work exceptionally well when they have protocols and constraints – structure – in which to work. Complete freedom can sometimes feel like a vacuum that drains the air out of teams. In our work with teams, both coaching and workshops, we experiment with a hypothesis that teams need structure to help them self-organise. We invite participants to self-organise around a task – usually some sort of learning activity. Here's what we find in group activities:

- Individuals become disoriented – often asking, 'what do you want to us do?' or 'what are we meant to be doing?'
- It takes a longer time to get the activity underway because time is taken up trying to establish 'rules'.
- Choosing who to work with takes on meaning – 'who shall I pick' or 'which group shall I join?'
- In debriefs, individuals often cite the chaos at the beginning as a demotivator.

Conversely, when we choose who will be in which group, give them clear instructions about how to do the task and create a timebox for them to do the work, the groups seem more comfortable.

This approach isn't a scientific experiment, but research suggests certain conditions under which teams tend to perform best when self-organising Eoyang (2001). Further insights from Buffer realised that structure is not synonymous with hierarchy.

Knowing what's working already

In their quest to become a Teal organisation Laloux (2014), that is, where employees self-manage and grow as the organisation grows, Buffer's enthusiasm led them to discount what was working already. Interestingly, Buurtzorg's adoption of a solution-focused approach to coaching means that they automatically consider what's working. Recognising an earlier assertion that apathy is our default state when met with challenges, it is easy to see how Buffer's early experiences of self-management floundered. Discussing the outcomes of their self-management experiment, Seiter (October 2015) explores with the two founders the lessons they learned. Here's a paraphrased list of what the essential learnings were:

- The importance of providing one on one support in the form of mentoring
- The value of stable teams – to bring focus to a longer-term vision
- The value of metrics as a means of providing guideposts and context for the work to be done
- Interdependency through making expectations clear – for this, they learned from Morning Star – another self-managed organisation that uses something called Colleague Letters of Understanding. Essentially explicit agreements about what your colleagues can expect from you and what you can expect from them.

While none of these examples specifically relate to coaching teams, they underpin the importance of unintended consequences. Knowing when to let go requires us to understand the broader landscape on which we coach teams. During the discovery phase, part of our due diligence is to help qualify the organisation and explore whether team coaching will help. If you're coaching a team and finding that the system is all too present in the room, we are responsible to the team to explore that dynamic. And help the teamwork out how they will navigate the organisational context. Asking what the stakeholders want from the team is an essential first step in the discovery process. Helping the stakeholders articulate this is crucial in discovering the focus for the coaching. We are revisiting this both during and after the coaching assignment to keep the stakeholders in the room. It also helps provide some of the structure mentioned earlier and introduces another level of accountability for the team.

Checking your ego at the door

The other trap we can fall into is our ego. It's flattering when teams want us to stay, and if we work as external coaches, it also means we have a regular income stream. If you've been working with a team for an extended period, the chances are you will have become socialised within the team's system. In other words, you will naturally start to fall into patterns of behaviour that might not serve the team. Additionally, the team will also begin to view you as a quasi-member of the team. Becoming seen as part of the team makes it harder to challenge the team's thinking and create tension within the team – particularly if solid interpersonal relationships develop. We should constantly guard against this and seek external supervision to check and balance what might be happening at a psycho-dynamic level.

When we leave our ego behind, we can ask more salient questions. In Eoyang's research (2001), it's clear that some teams didn't need to be a team. We can also help the team understand what type of team they need to be in the future. We work with the organisation when we work with the team. The team merely mirrors the organisational system. As we've seen already, in the case of Buurtzorg, this is an elegant dance between the team and the broader ecosystem they support.

7.4 Letting come – knowing what's next

The final piece of the jigsaw puzzle is where we help the team develop a plan for progress. Ideally, this should be in conjunction with the team's stakeholders. We've often started the conversation around a continuing development plan from the initial meeting in one-on-one coaching. This continuing development plan asks the client what they want to achieve, their goals, hopes and dreams and how the coaching will make a difference. At the final session, after the retrospective review, we start to help them plan what next. How they do this is their choice, we help them construct a meaningful transition from coaching to self-coaching. Many years ago, I remembered feeling bereft when my final coaching session ended with my coach. I wasn't sure what I would do and how I would cope without my regular coaching conversations. They helped me navigate some tricky and stressful work situations, and I had become, unwittingly, reliant on my coach. With her help, I realised I had learned so many different strategies I was ready to 'go it alone'.

We should be mindful of how the team might be feeling as we work towards liberating their potential and encouraging them to self-coach. A gradual process of handover, as we've mentioned, is therefore essential. The coaching assignment can be represented in the following way in Figure 7.1.

Each session presents an opportunity for the team to learn more about how they coach themselves. And gradually, by the final session, the team should be coaching each other with you and your fellow coach taking a sidestep outside the coaching circle. In the first session, you and the team will likely have created some coaching manifesto. The final session reviews the manifesto to see what's changed, what's been added and how much progress the team has made. Part 2 of this activity is helping the team identify gaps in their development they can take forward together as a coaching team. Figure 7.2 is a suggested framework

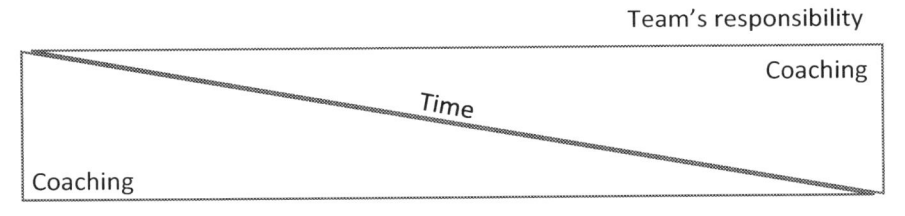

Figure 7.1 Gradual Transition of Coaching Responsibility

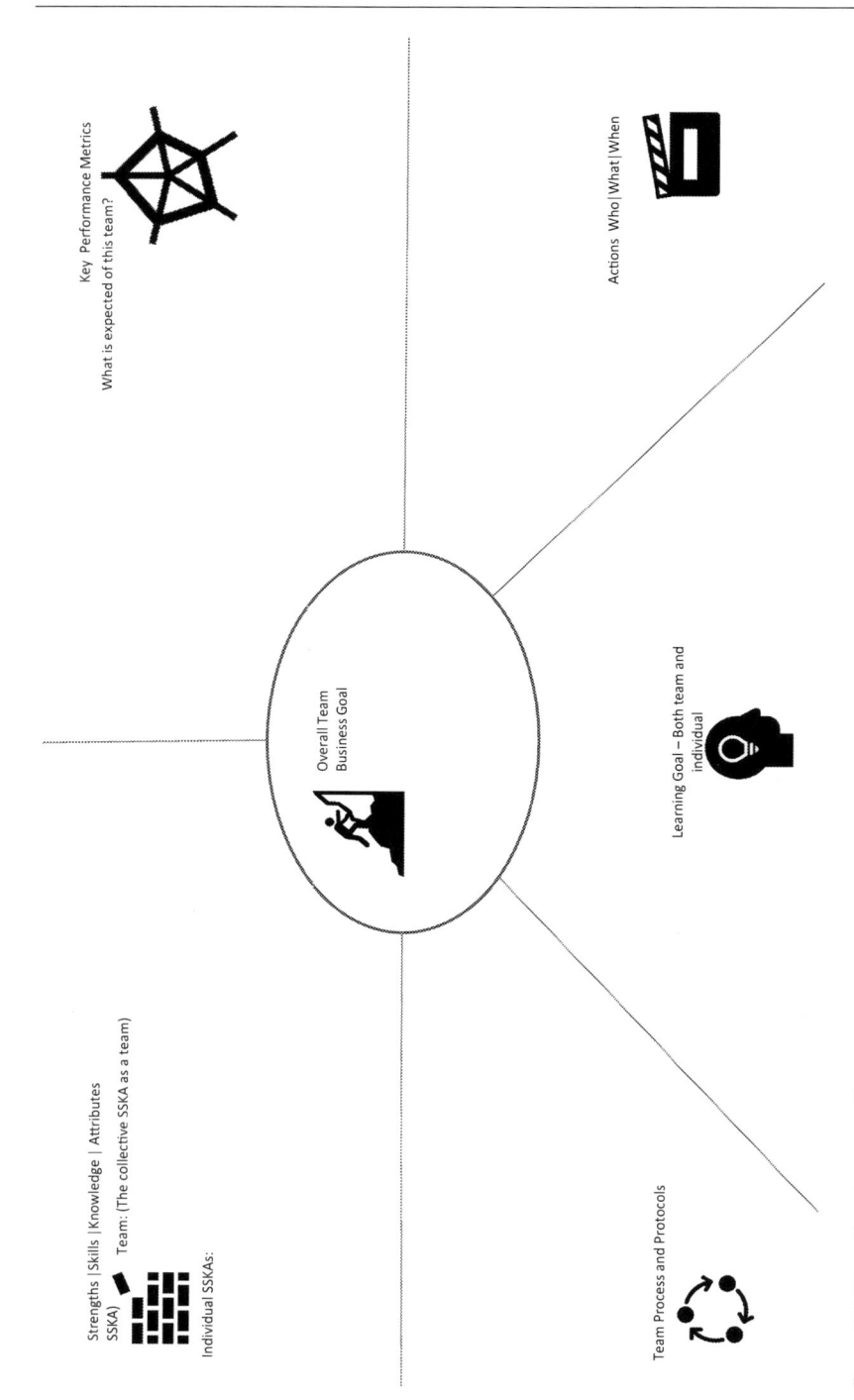

Figure 7.2 Team Development Canvas

you can use to help visualise what needs to be done and prompt questions to help populate the plan.

The team can choose a method of doing this for themselves. As we've established, though, sometimes it's helpful to have a loose structure the team can start with and create their own from there. We've already seen some of the tools for coaching teams in a previous chapter, go back and look at the Team Effectiveness Review for some ideas for questions to ask. For example,

- How well does the team observe what's happening in the sessions?
- How proactive are they at initiating conversations?
- How do they listen to each other? Is it peripheral or deep level listening?
- How willing is the team to experiment?
- How well do they collaborate?

Ask the team which questions they need to ask each other to create a great team development plan. Explore with the team what they might need to let go of or unlearn to develop new team habits. Ask the team to come up with a list of areas they potentially could create. A list of potential topics is given in Table 7.2 to use as examples if necessary.

Table 7.2 Topics for Team Development Discussion

Topics for inclusion in Team Development Discussion
Business skills
Conflict and tough conversations
How to give and receive feedback
Negotiation skills
Coaching skills
Team protocols
Collegiate working
Observation skills
Questioning skills
Listening skills
Stakeholder engagement
Networking
Continuous improvement
Team learning
Diversity
Innovation
Team health
Teaming Skills

Ideally, the team should come up with their list. There may well be technical skills on the list that relate to their specific context. For example, at Buurtzorg, the core role is nursing, so some nursing aspects will likely feature on their team development plan.

Planning is more important than 'the plan'

All plans are only relevant until they make the first contact with the customer or stakeholder. Upon the first contact, the plan will likely change. Similarly, any change in the context will also have implications for the plan. The team should review their plan every quarter to see what is still relevant, what has been achieved already and what needs to renovate. Or a timeframe that makes sense for the team. We discussed a mid-point review earlier and for non-project teams. Reviewing team development at set intervals provides a neat cycle for conducting retrospectives and updates on the team development plan. For stable teams that have worked together for long periods, creating an opportunity to refresh their skills and check in with each other on progress can re-invigorate the team. Irrespective, the team needs to make the developmental process meaningful for them and one in which everyone can engage. Working with other teams or swapping team members around with other teams on planned secondments provides cross-fertilisation opportunities across the organisation. It also enables teams to cross-pollinate ideas and share work practices that might help each other. Short-term and project teams have an advantage for organisations in that their learning can be spread quickly to other teams as they form and re-form. The downside is that speed of change can sometimes mean the learning and team development process is secondary to the team task and can put to one side. If the team doesn't have learning at a conscious level, the teams will potentially fall back onto old ways of working.

Helping the team focus on 'what next?' is essential for the team. It's also vital for the coach or coaches too. Will you, for example, do a follow-up visit with the team in a few months to hear how they're doing? I often check in with teams to see what's happened since we last met. It provides an opportunity for me to learn what helped the team. It also helps create an elegant ending and the possibility of a new beginning.

7.5 Chapter summary

Knowing when to quit is an essential tenet in coaching. It's not easy to say goodbye to a team, especially when you've got to know the team members at a deep level.

- Coaching is a short-term intervention. We should be transparent on the duration of the coaching assignment and work towards exiting the team before it becomes reliant on us.
- Scoping and discovery help identify what the team will work on and the likely time required to help them make progress.

- Transition the team to a fully functional self-organising system is the purpose of team coaching.
- Retrospectives and pre-mortems support the habit of continuous improvement. Furthermore, it creates a thinking environment for deeper level learning and decision making.
- Coach self-reflection is an essential part of team coaching. The coach should attend to their learning as much as the team. In this way, the coach models good practice. Change is a natural part of life, and coaches need to be flexible and adapt to the changing makeup of teams. Having approaches for helping teams cope with membership change is part of this progress. Teams are dynamic living systems.
- There are many organisations following a self-organising model. Buurtzorg is one of the best known. It provides a learning resource for teams seeking self-organisation. It also demonstrates how success can be linked with self-organisation.
- There is no prescriptive model for self-organisation, and companies like Buffer have followed an experimental approach that led to their current model. Teams and coaches should be open to experimentation.
- A solution-focused approach helps the team focus on what's working already. Identifying what the team did to create their current level of performance gives confidence that they can move the needle even further.
- Ego-free coaching is a must when working with teams. Adopting curiosity as a mantra helps keep us grounded and open to taking the team to where it needs to go.
- Passing the baton regularly and deliberately means that we are constantly transitioning the team from being coached to being coaches. Our strategy is to leave the team in an even better place and capable of self-coaching.

Bibliography

Bennis, W. G., and Shepard, H. A. (1956) A Theory of Group Development. *Human Relations*, vol. 9, no. 4, pp. 415–437. https://doi.org/10.1177/001872675600900403.

Edmondson, A. C., and Harvey, J. (2017) *Extreme Teaming: Lesson in Complex, Cross-Sector Leadership*. Bingley, UK: Emerald Publishing.

Eoyang, G. H. (2001) Conditions for Self-Organizing in Human Systems. *Human Systems Dynamics Institute*. https://www.hsdinstitute.org/resources/conditions-for-self-organizing-in-human-systems.html. Accessed October 28, 2020.

Falk, D. (1995) Preflection: A Strategy for Enhancing Reflection. *Evaluation/Reflection*, 22. Centre for Public Impact. https://digitalcommons.unomaha.edu/slceeval/22.

Gersick, C. (1988) Time and Transition in Work Teams: Toward a New Model of Group Development. *Academy of Management Journal*, vol. 31, no. 1. https://doi.org/10.2307/256496. Accessed April 18, 2021.

Hamel, G. (2011) First, Let's Fire All the Managers. *Harvard Business Review*. https://hbr.org/2011/12/first-lets-fire-all-the-managers. Accessed April 18, 2021.

Jones, G., and Gorell, R. (2021) *50 Top Tools for Coaching = A Complete Toolkit for Developing and Empowering People*. London: Kogan Page.

Kaloudis, H. (2016) *A Systematic Overview of the Literature in English on Buurtzorg Nederland: Part B – The Buurtzorg Organisational and Operational Model.* Medium Article. https://medium.com/@Harri_Kaloudis/a-systematic-overview-of-the-literature-in-english-on-buurtzorg-nederland-part-b-the-buurtzorg-189a7e4704b0. Accessed April 20, 2021.

Kirkpatrick, D. (2017) *Beyond Empowerment: The Age of the Self-Managed Organization.* Jetlaunch.

Laloux, F. (2014) *Reinventing Organizations*, Illustrated edition. Nelson Parker.

Mcgrath, J. E. (1991) Time, Interaction, and Performance (TIP): A Theory of Groups. *Small Group Research*, vol. 22, no. 2, pp. 147–174. https://doi.org/10.1177/1046496491222001.

Nandram, S. (2015) *Organizational Innovation by Integrating Simplification – Learning from Buurtzorg Nederland.* Switzerland: Springer International Publishing.

Schein, E. (1999) *Process Consultation Revisited: Building the Helping Relationship.* Reading, MA: Addison-Wesley Publishing Company, Inc.

Seiter, C. (2015) *Self Defined Self-Management: How Our Startup Is Figuring It Out Together.* https://buffer.com/resources/self-management-circle/. Accessed April 20, 2021.

Tuckman, B. (1965) Developmental Sequence in Small Groups. *Psychological Bulletin*, vol. 63, pp. 384–399.

Wenting, B. (2013) *Buurtzorg Meeting Part 1.* YouTube Channel. https://youtu.be/ff-FRhO5QmM. Accessed April 20, 2021.

Wenting, B. (2013) *Buurtzorg Meeting Part 2.* YouTube Channel. https://youtu.be/Ay41B7Z4HxE. Accessed April 20, 2021.

Wenting, B. (2013) *Buurtzorg Meeting Part 3.* YouTube Channel. https://youtu.be/35RhQ8s1rVQ. Accessed April 20, 2021.

Widrich, L. (2015) *What We Got Wrong about Self-management: Embracing Natural Hierarchy at Work.* https://buffer.com/resources/self-management-hierarchy/.

Chapter 8

Conclusions and next steps

We started this journey by posing some declarative statements, which we'll review in this final chapter.

- Teams are collections of independent members: teams are interdependent.
- Self-organising teams don't just happen on their own.
- Teams often fall into the trap of groupthink.
- Working through conflict is healthy if teams are to succeed.
- Team coaching tools and techniques can be learnt.
- Adaptability is a learned skill. Resilience helps flex the muscle.
- All good things come to an end.
- Self-organising teams aren't for everyone.

A shared task and mission link teams by necessity; if the linkage isn't there, the team doesn't exist. Organisations often miss this point and expect to leverage performance from teams, yet no glue binds the people together. The overriding reason for working together is missing. Self-organisation requires this glue more so than other types of teams. The metaphor of the hive is even more fitting when we think of self-organising teams. Purpose and shared responsibility for results are paramount in defining the team.

Self-organisation is a continuum – determined by how much power the team has to decide their path. How far down the path of self-governing the organisation is willing to go determines whether the team is autonomous or not. Due diligence on whether self-organising teams are appropriate for your organisation is key.

A necessary part of team working is the ability to be open and robust. Healthy debate and confronting tricky issues are essential if teams are to do their best work. Healthy debate can only be possible if there is psychological safety. Trust among team members helps create a cohesive unit willing to have each other's backs and work towards a shared goal. The team needs to have ways to cope with disagreements and pathways for effective decision making. Buurtzorg is an excellent example of how the team is set up for success.

One of the potential reasons for Buurtzorg's success is effective boundary management. The scope of the roles within the team is narrow – the core technical

DOI: 10.4324/9781003110583-9

competency in nursing. In other self-organising teams, for example, Buffer, the teams have a variety of skillsets. Part of Buurtzorg's success could be argued is down to narrowness of scope. Yes, the nurses are required to share other responsibilities, but the core skill set is nursing. The second fact is the explicit constraints the team works within. There are set productivity levels and the teams operate within a defined geographical neighbourhood – so there is no internal competition. The teams are also linked to the community they serve – they have direct access to key stakeholders. They are responsible for developing their care practice based on networking and building client lists.

It is easy to argue that following the approach of Buurtzorg might lead to a greater chance of success. However, as we know, organisations are complex systems. What we can take from a study of Buurtzorg are things that we know help teams work more effectively together. There are clear roles and responsibilities, and they have protocols to help make decisions. Regional coaches support the teams, and they are trained in coaching and business skills; there is an infrastructure that supports the teams, such as Buurtzorg technology. We can learn from this example that the purpose behind self-organisation is thorough and links with the overarching purpose and mission to help create independent living for its clients.

Self-organising teams work well if there is a compelling reason for the organisation to adopt this model. In their book on Humanocracy (2020), Hamel and Zanini explore many different organisations that have moved away from a hierarchical model to one where individuals and team are given autonomy. Haier is one of the organisations they reference and of particular interest is a subsidiary of GE that Haier acquired. If your organisation moves from a hierarchical to a more self-organised model, it will likely take time. It is challenging to adopt a model that requires a 180-degree pivot.

Coaching self-organising teams to become vanguards of a new way of working in your organisation is one way of transitioning to a different model. What would you advise organisations? I posed this question to the people I interviewed. One piece of advice that stood out was this. If you're a large corporate organisation, find somewhere that is not working well. Start there. What's the worst that could happen? Chances are that it will improve from where you are currently.

There is nothing more rewarding than working with a team and see them flourish and enjoying each other's company. In 2020, I was lucky enough to be part of a self-organising team. We didn't have a coach, but we coached each other. There were some highs and lows, and we delivered on what we promised, had some fun and had a team member change. Whilst I have focused on coaching self-organising teams, it goes without saying that the best way to learn is by experiencing being a part of a self-organising team yourself.

I leave you with the coaching principles as a reminder to start with these – or your own. And I hope I've left you in a better place, confident to coach self-organising teams and leave them capable of coaching each other.

Prime Directive: leave the team capable of coaching itself

Guiding Principles:

We coach the team in the room and the organisation they represent – individual team members cannot know everything about the organisation. Collectively, the team will have a better understanding of the whole organisation. The parable of the blind men and elephant – each has a subjective experience of part of the elephant they touch, but none can describe how the whole elephant looks. We are prisoners of our subjective experiences, and only through discussion and exploration can we create an entire picture.

Coach the team on tangible business challenges first – our job is not to 'fix' the team. We assume the team can work effectively on business issues. Our role is to help discover ways of working that increase capability and capacity to improve these skills. In the process, we will help the team work together as a collective whole. They will have the ability to resolve theory issues and come up with solutions through the coaching process.

Focus on creating teaming skills – we coach the team to find better ways of making decisions, navigating conflict, working together and developing resilience to create and join other teams with ease. In the knowledge, they have resources on which to draw.

Assume the team can self-organise – all team members can make decisions and work productively with others given the support and delegated authority. Coach the team to identify their superpowers and help them navigate organisational challenges.

Solutions may not be apparent in only one session – coaching the team to discuss and think through issues might not lead to a ready solution. Sometimes the work happens between the sessions. Support the team in allowing the space for deeper thinking and help co-create processes that support an emergent approach to solution generation.

Deliberate practice requires action and retrospection – Support the team to practice what they are learning. Design into the coaching process the opportunity for the team to gradually assume responsibility for coaching each other. Create opportunities for reflection and insight for further experimentation.

Create a framework for collaboration – teamwork is about interdependence. Co-create how the team will work together and rely on each other collectively to attain their goal. Encourage individual self-discipline in the service of the team. Help the team co-create a powerful shared agenda.

Teams are complex systems, therefore experimentation is essential – there is no magic formula for working with teams. No process can adequately describe how you will work with each team. Whilst there might be some common themes, it is probable that each team will have a different way of combining those themes that creates a unique coaching experience. Tools and techniques are great to have in your toolkit, but the best tool is experimentation and curiosity.

Leave the team in a better place – a second directive of 'first do no harm' guides this final principle. We work with the team to create a supportive and motivating environment that they create for each other. Our goal is to start from where they are and help make it a little better each time we work with the team. We take a solution-focused approach to a future possible state in our coaching stance.

Bibliography

Hamel, G., and Zanini, M. (2020) Humanocracy: Creating Organizations as Amazing as the People Inside Them. Boston, MA: Harvard Business Review Press.

Index

Note: Page numbers in *italics* indicate a figure and page numbers in **bold** indicate a table on the corresponding page.

Printed in the United States
by Baker & Taylor Publisher Services